A A A A A A

A A A A A A

a a a a a a a

a a a a a a a

Aa Aa Aa Aa

Get more practice on the lines below.

Aa Aa Aa Aa

Aa Aa Aa Aa

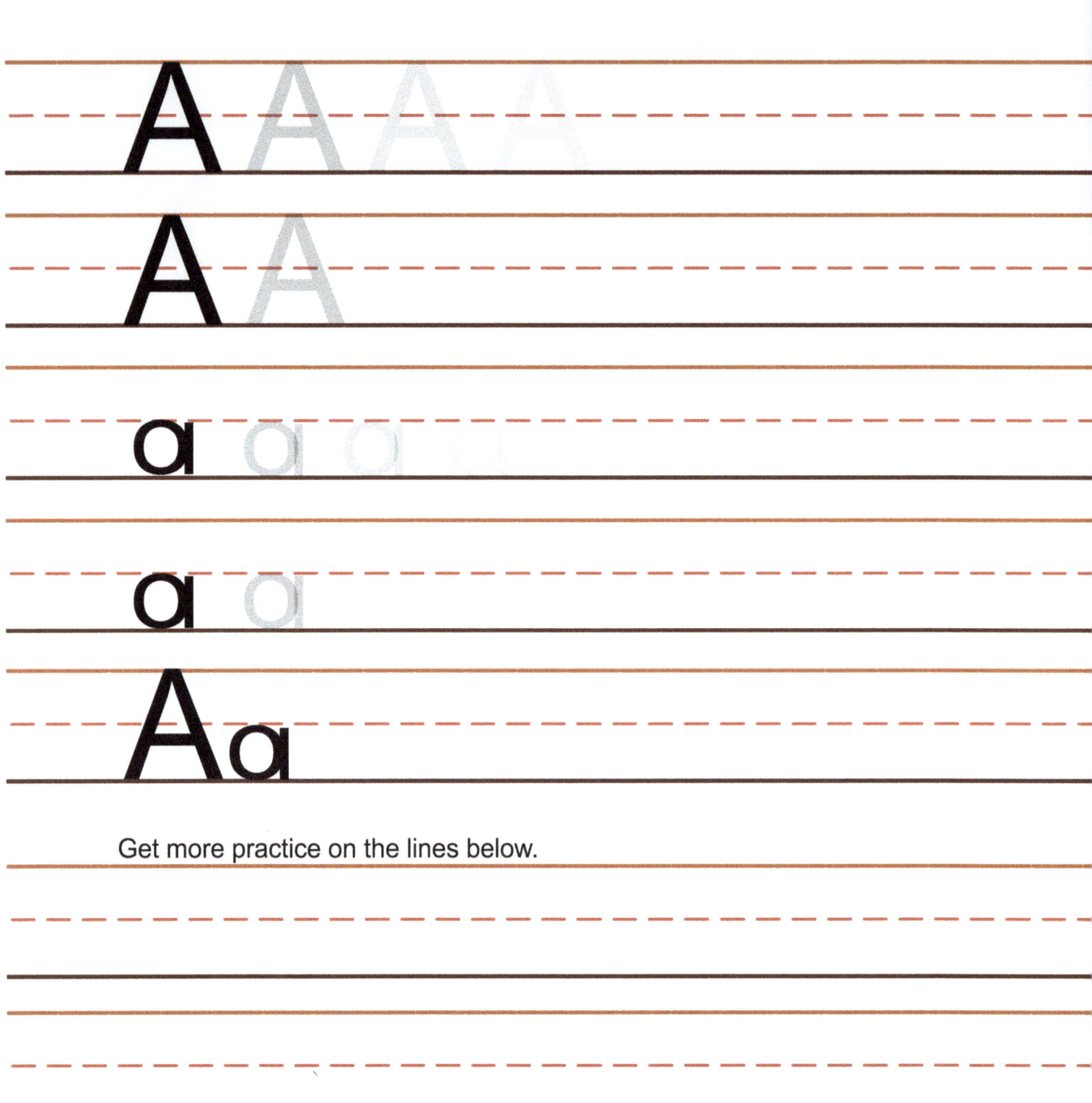

Get more practice on the lines below.

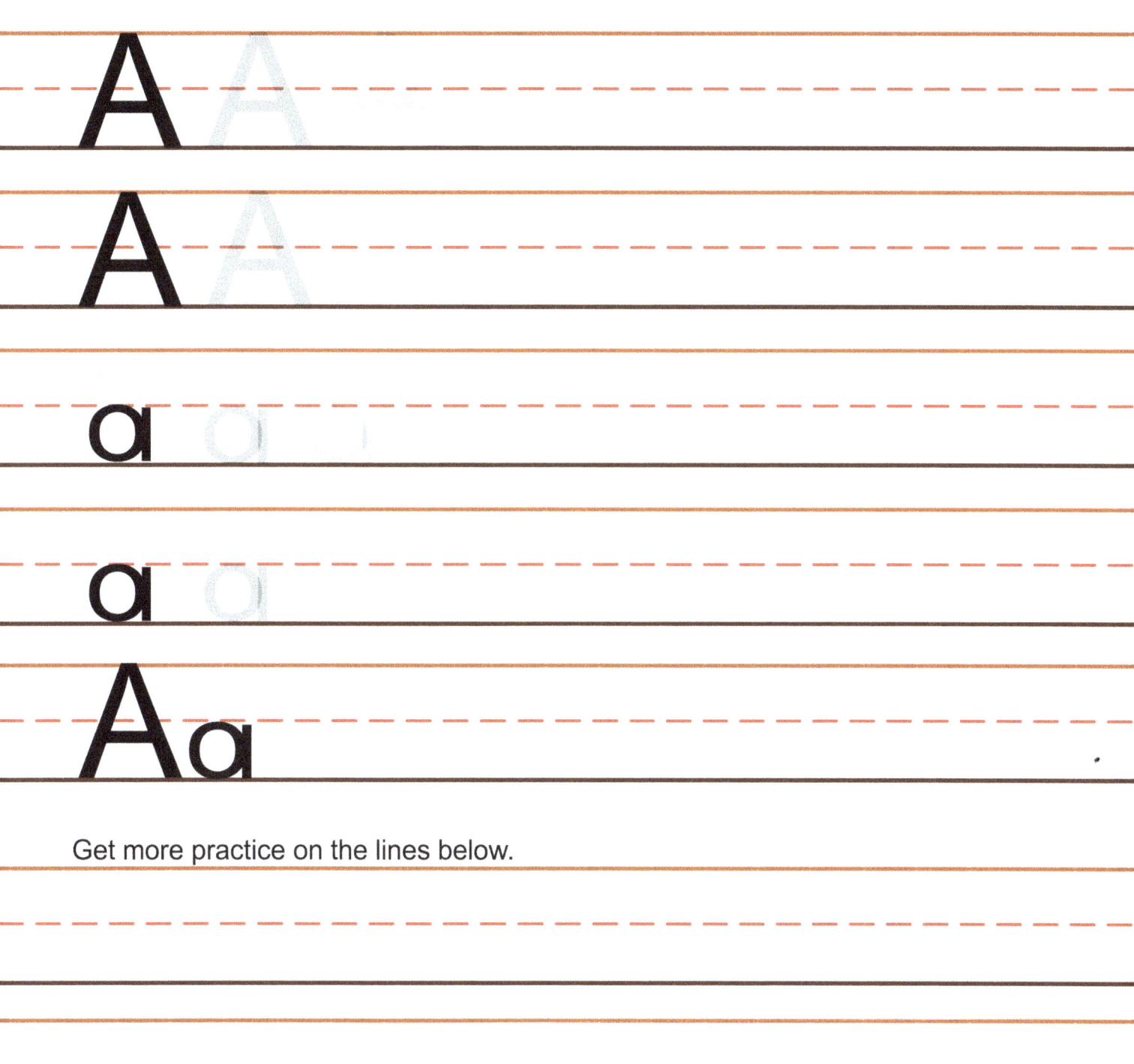

Get more practice on the lines below.

Color the letters.

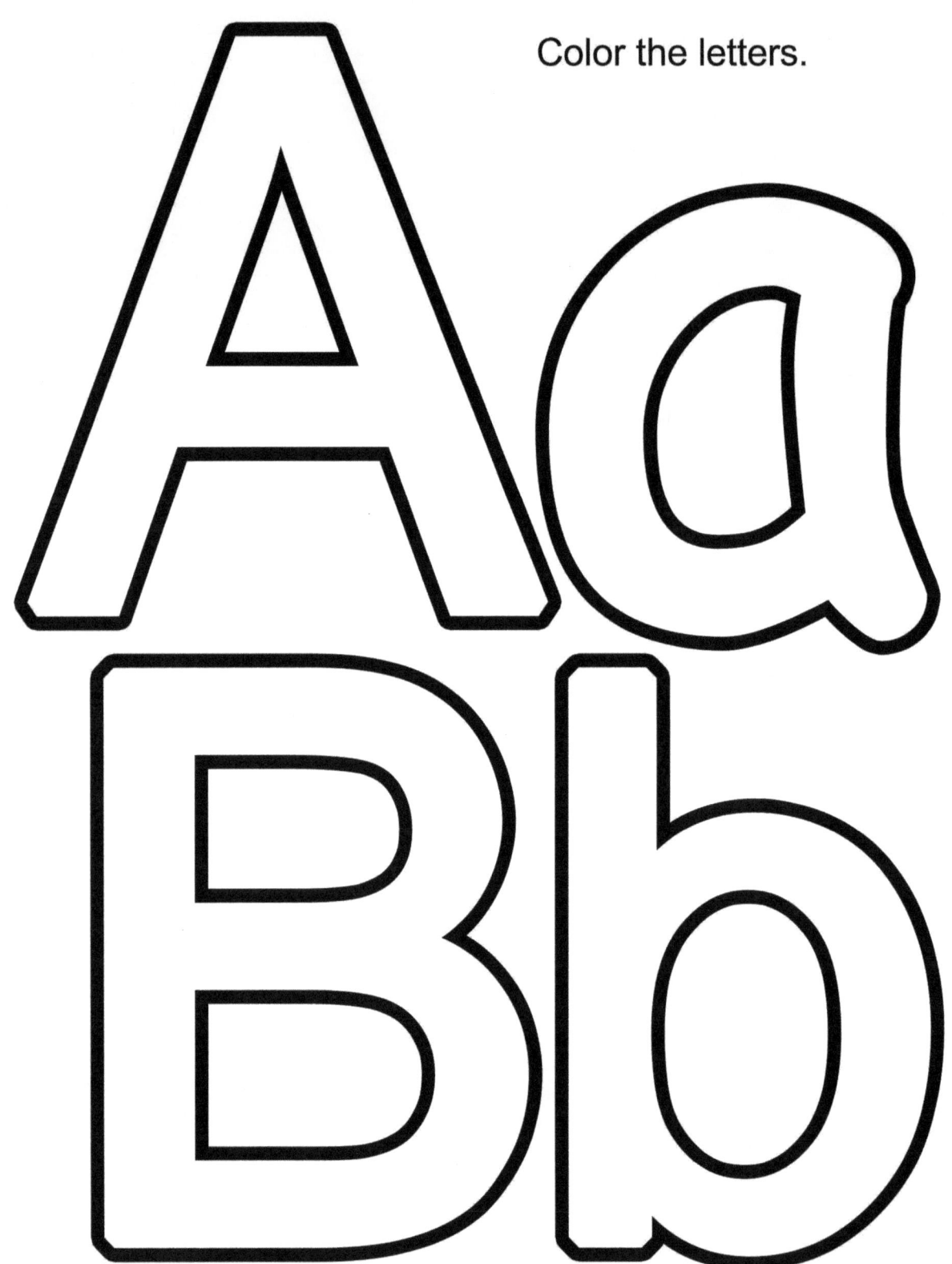

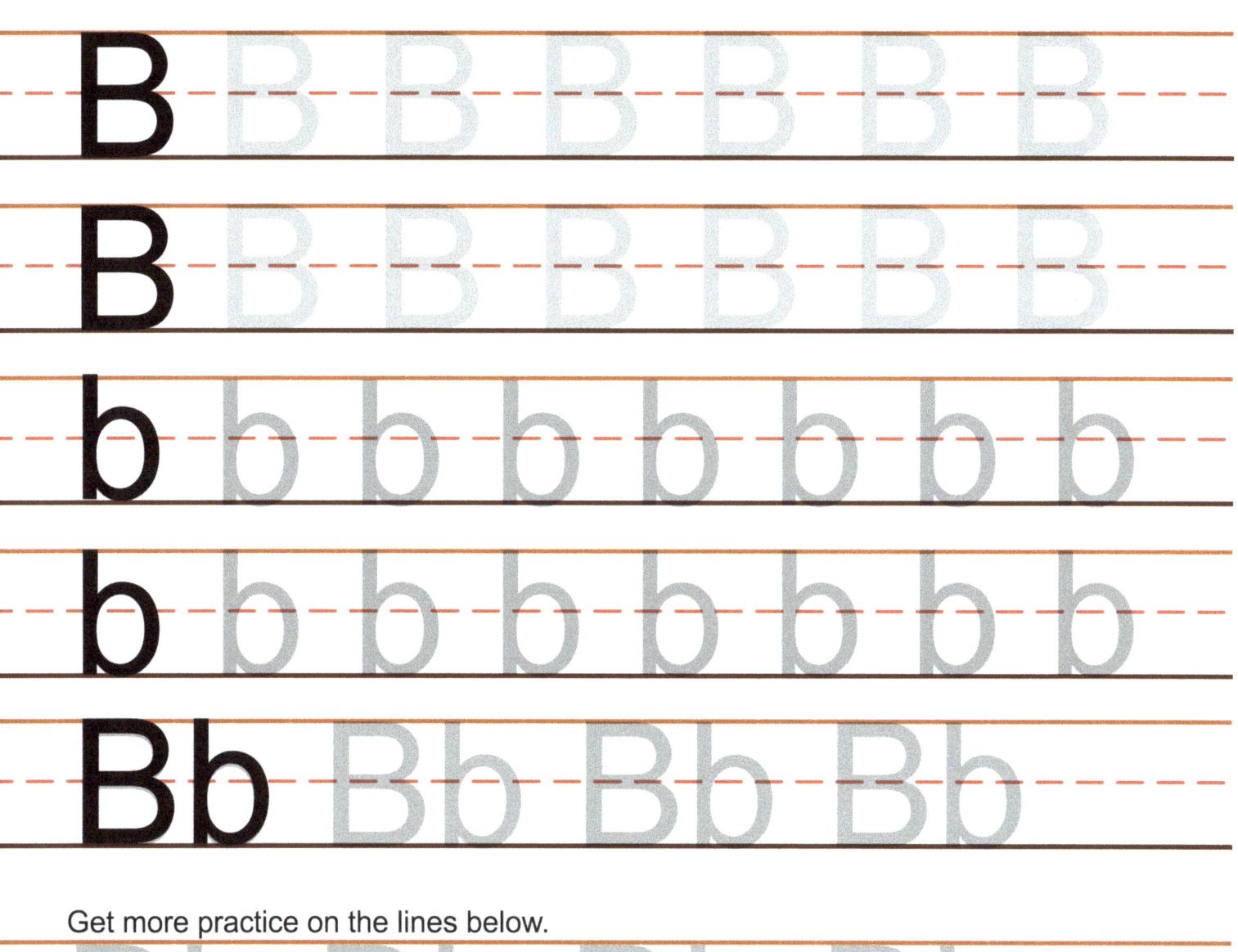

Get more practice on the lines below.

B B B B

B B

b b b

b b

Bb

Get more practice on the lines below.

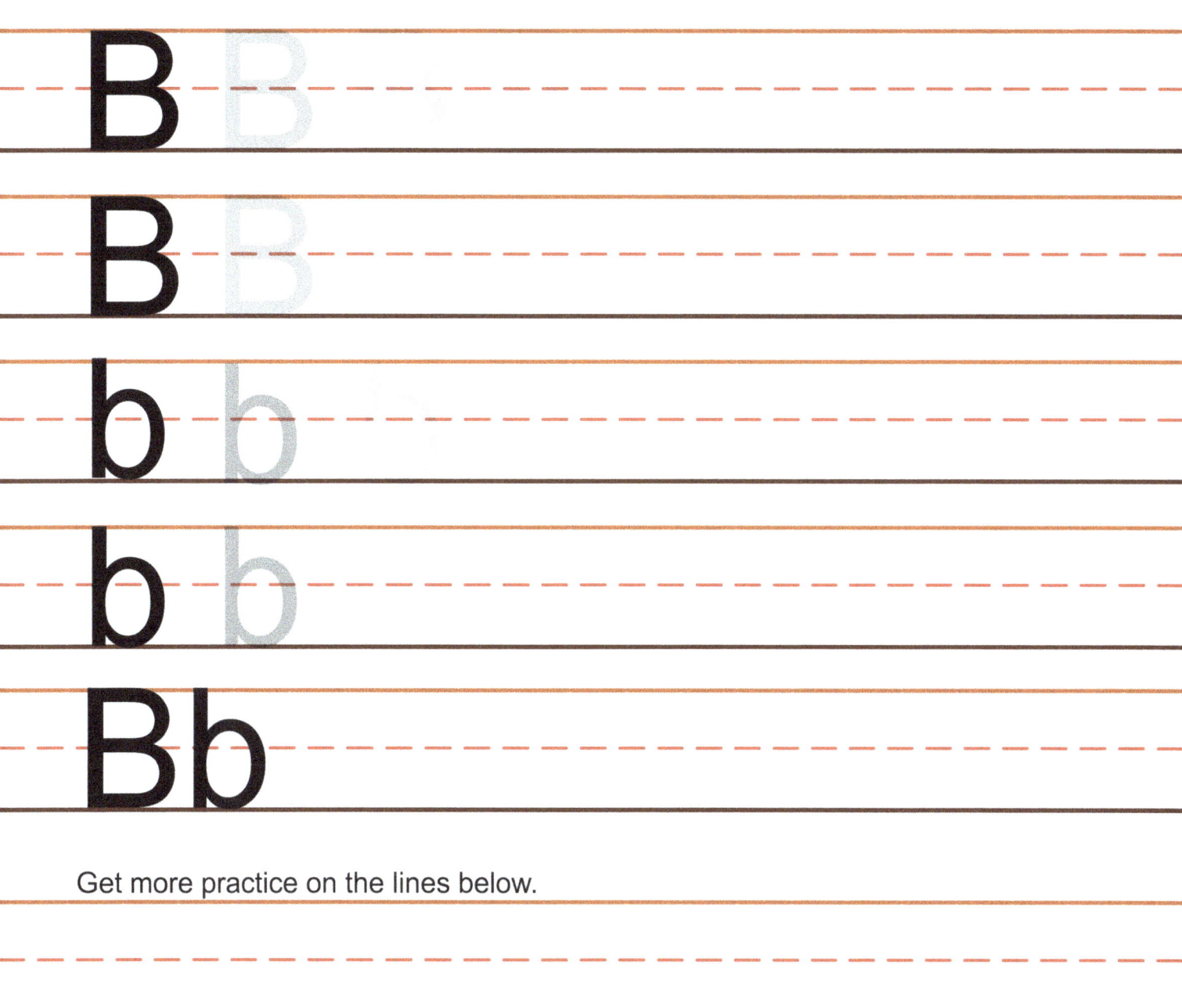

Get more practice on the lines below.

Color the letters.

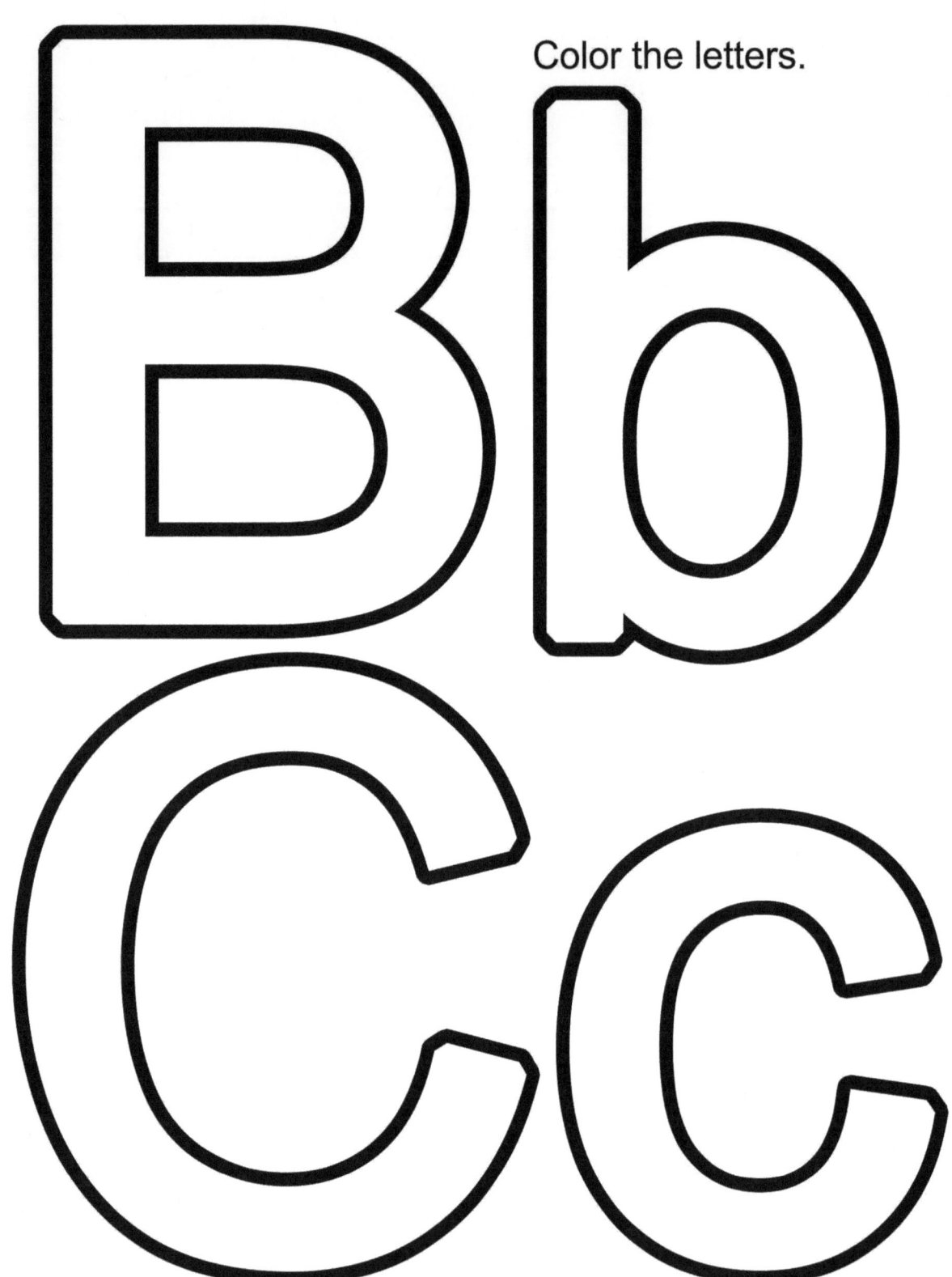

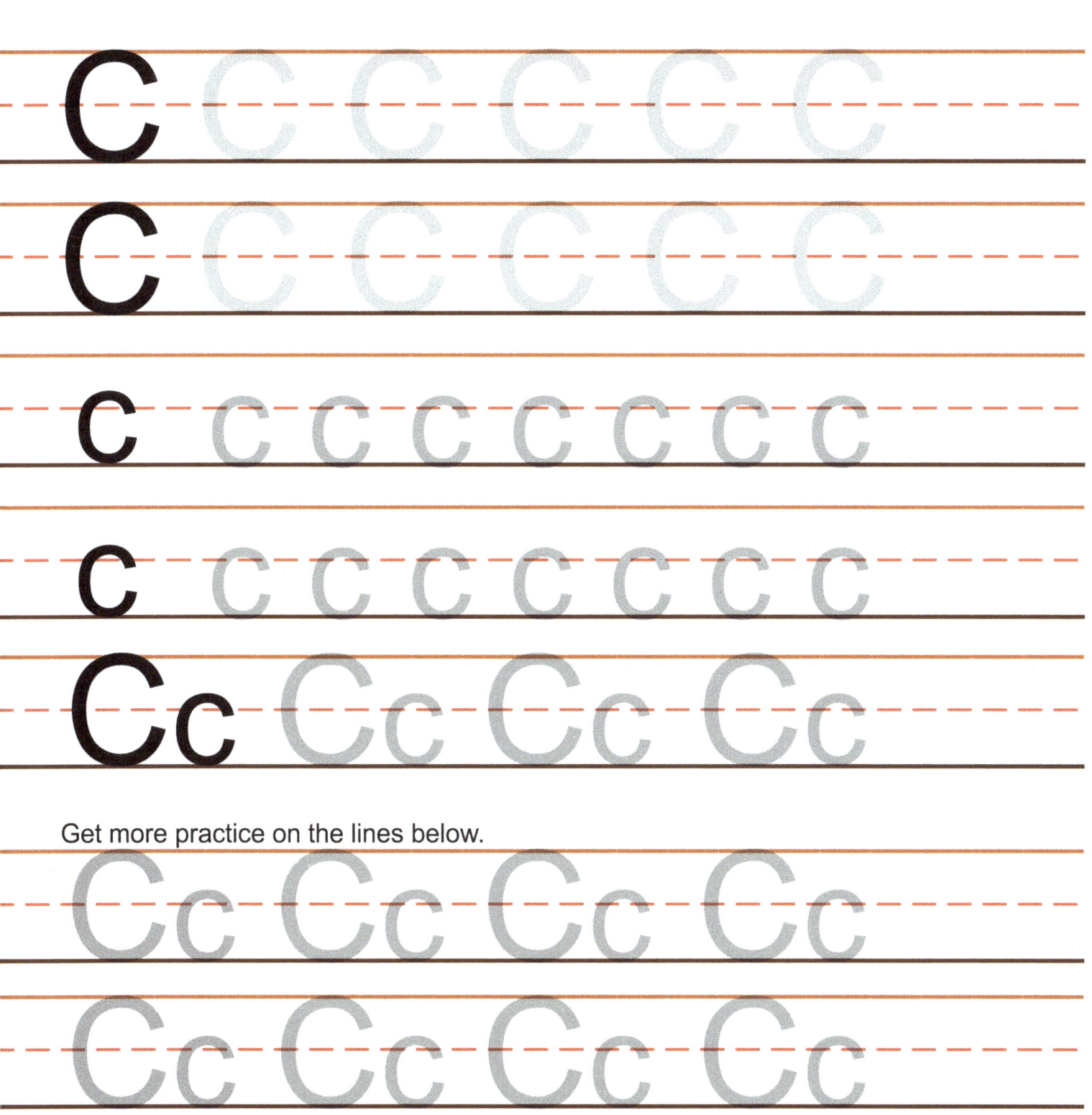

Get more practice on the lines below.

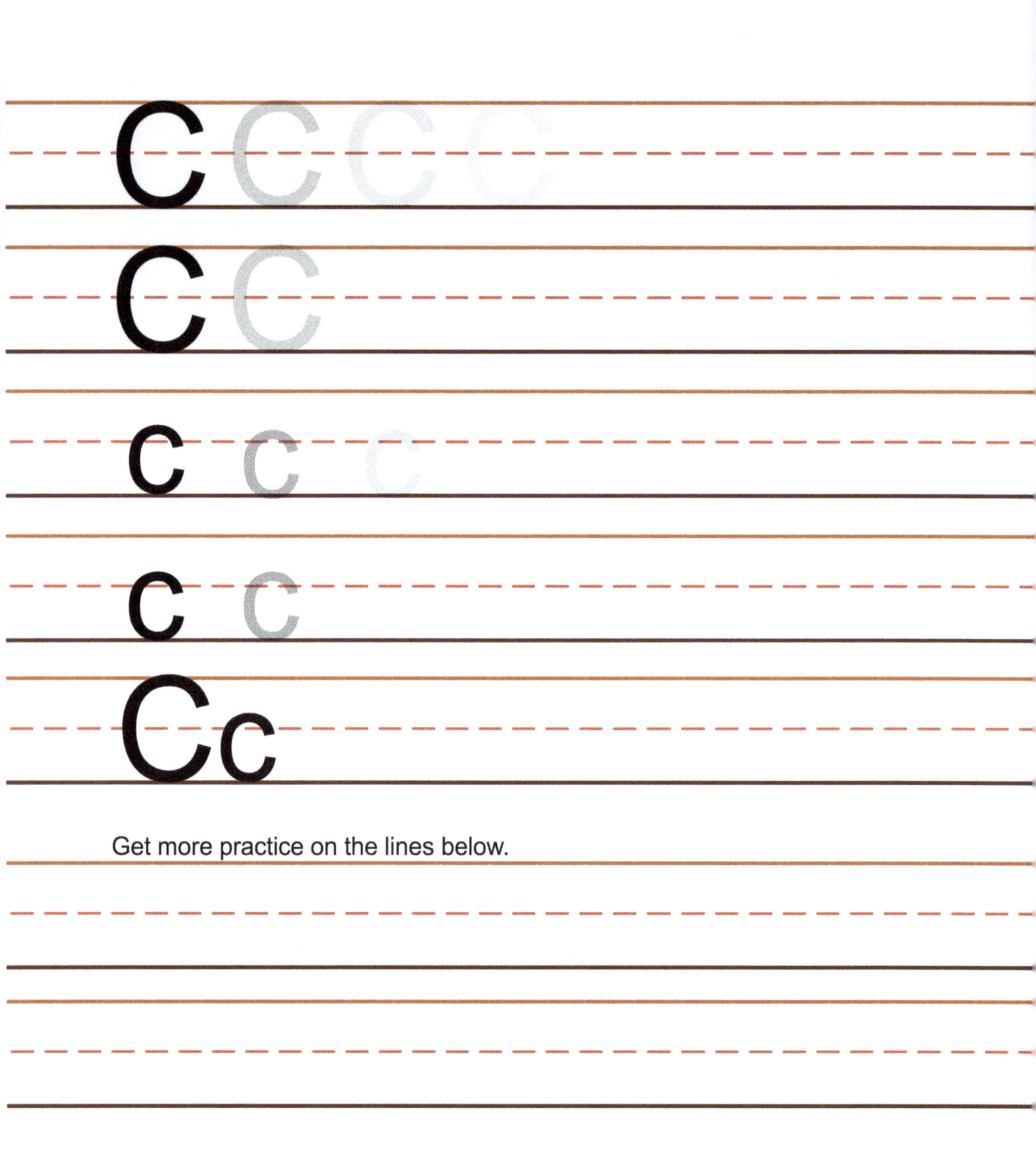

Get more practice on the lines below.

Get more practice on the lines below.

Color the letters.

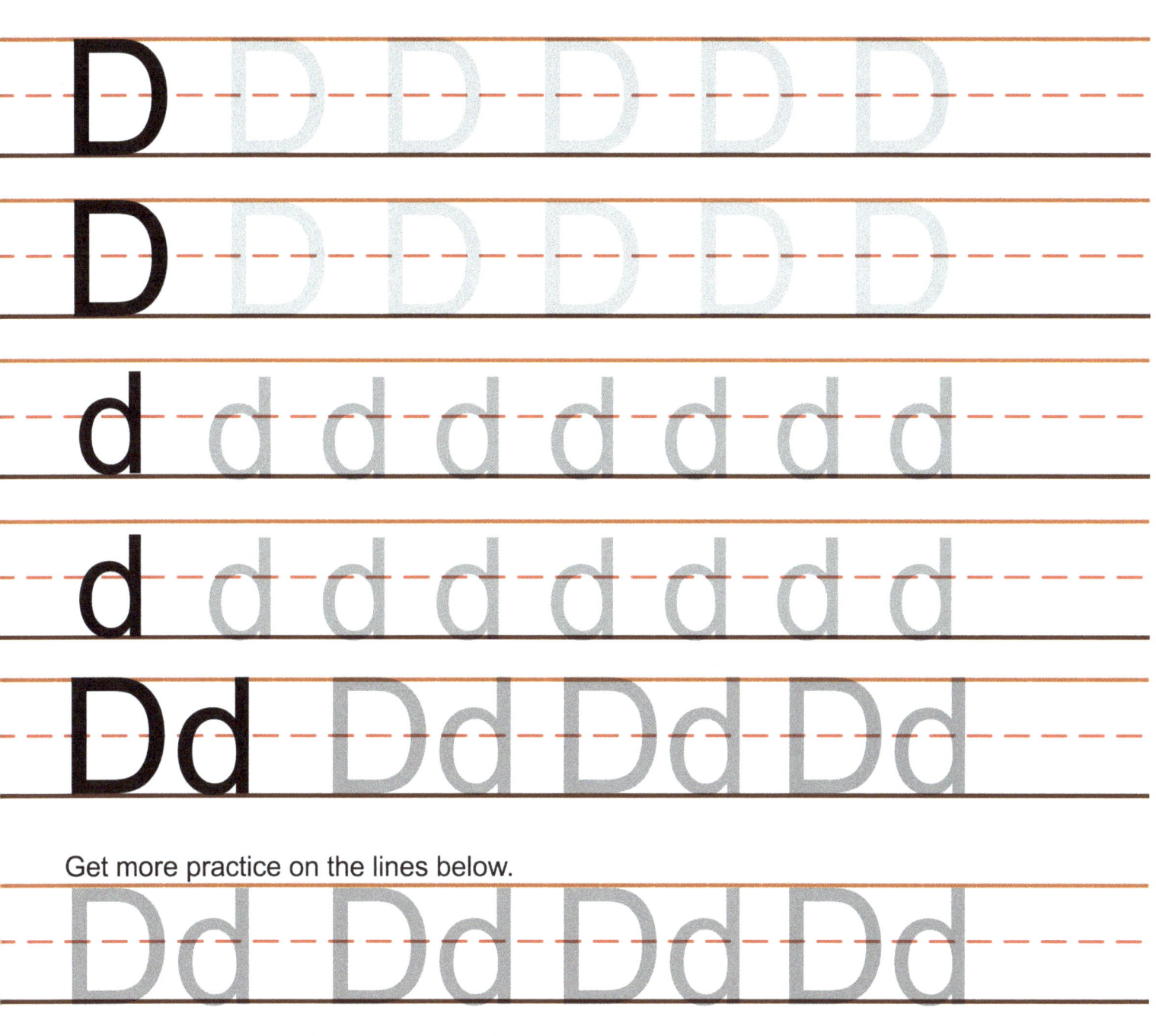

Get more practice on the lines below.

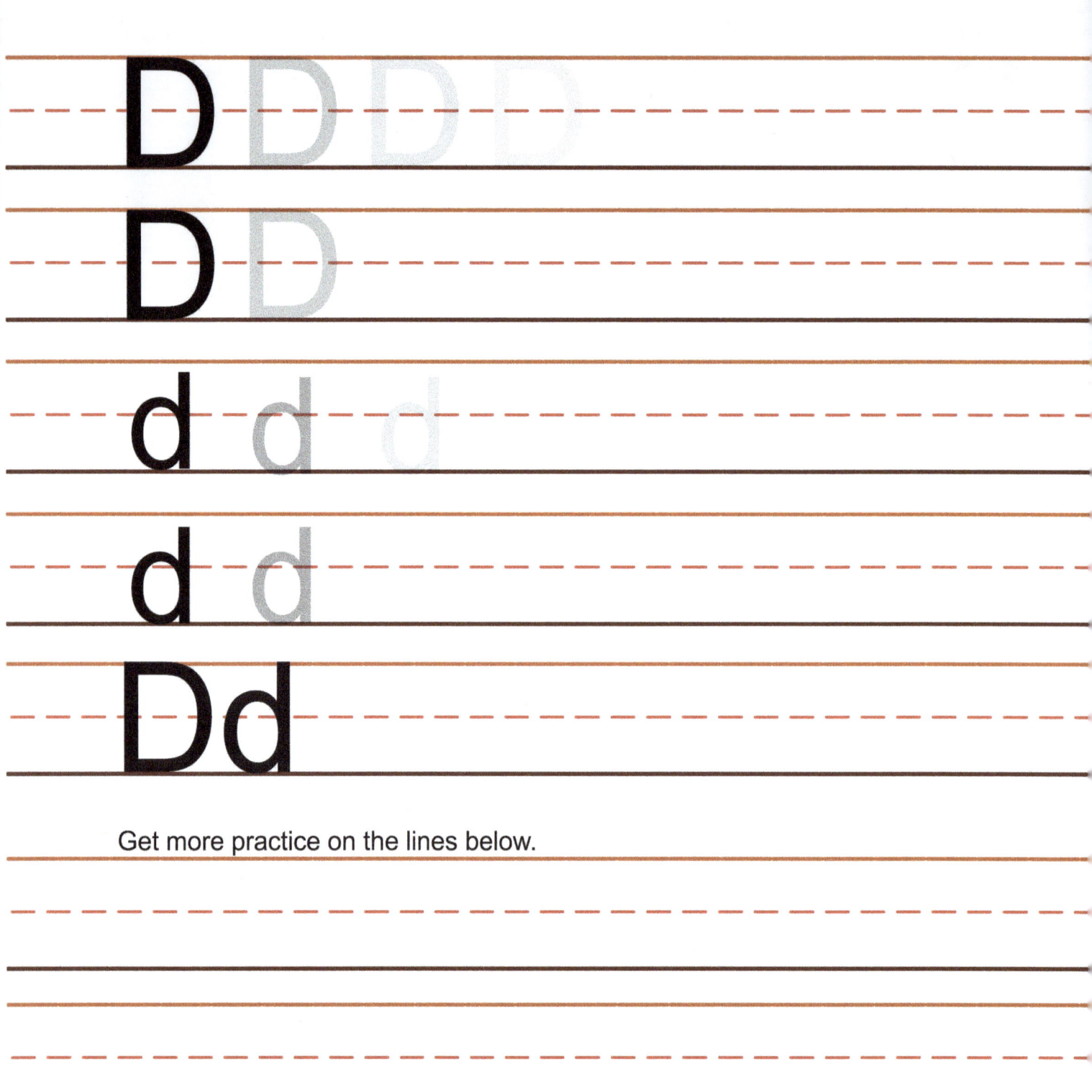

Get more practice on the lines below.

Get more practice on the lines below.

Color the letters.

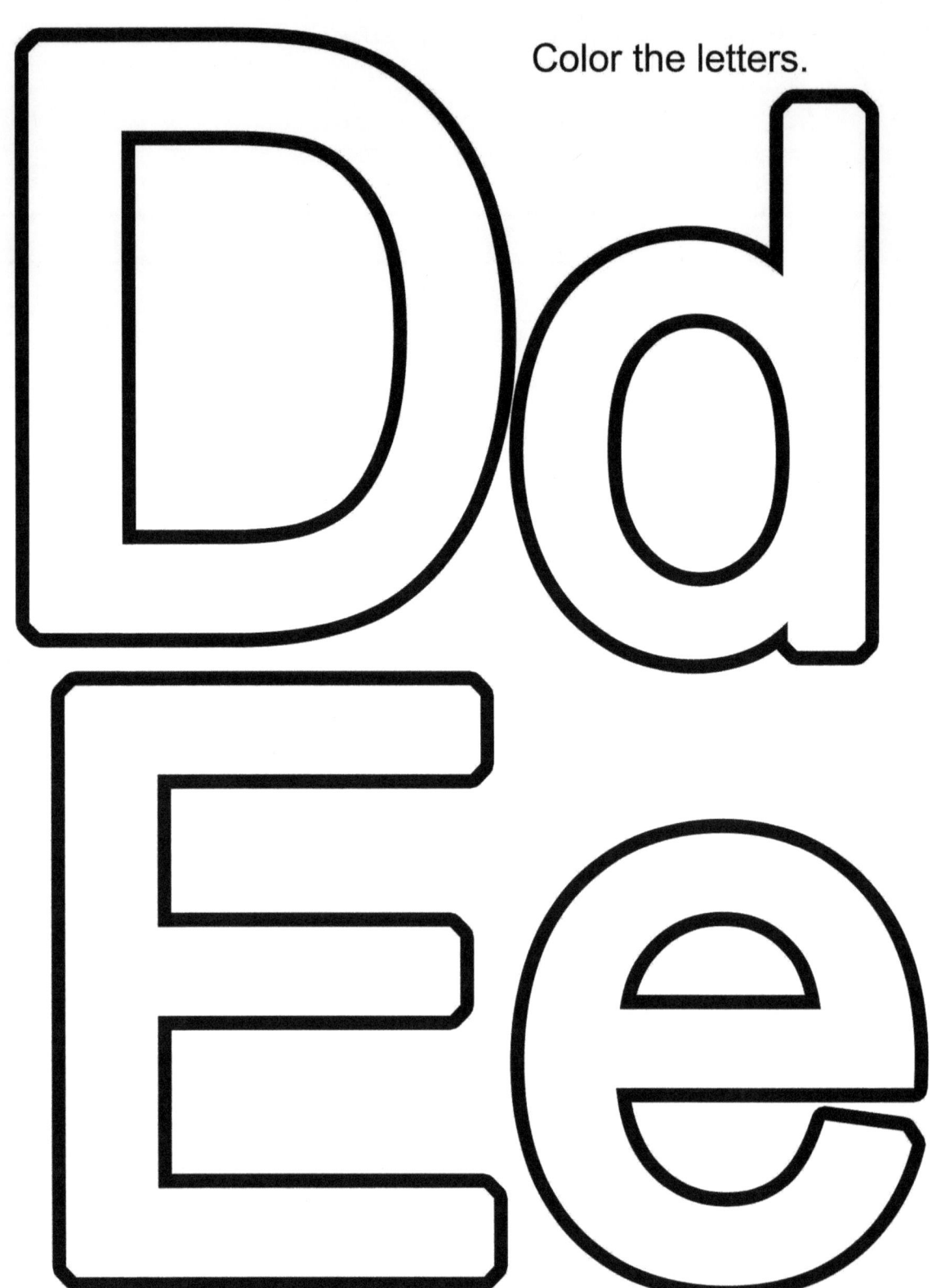

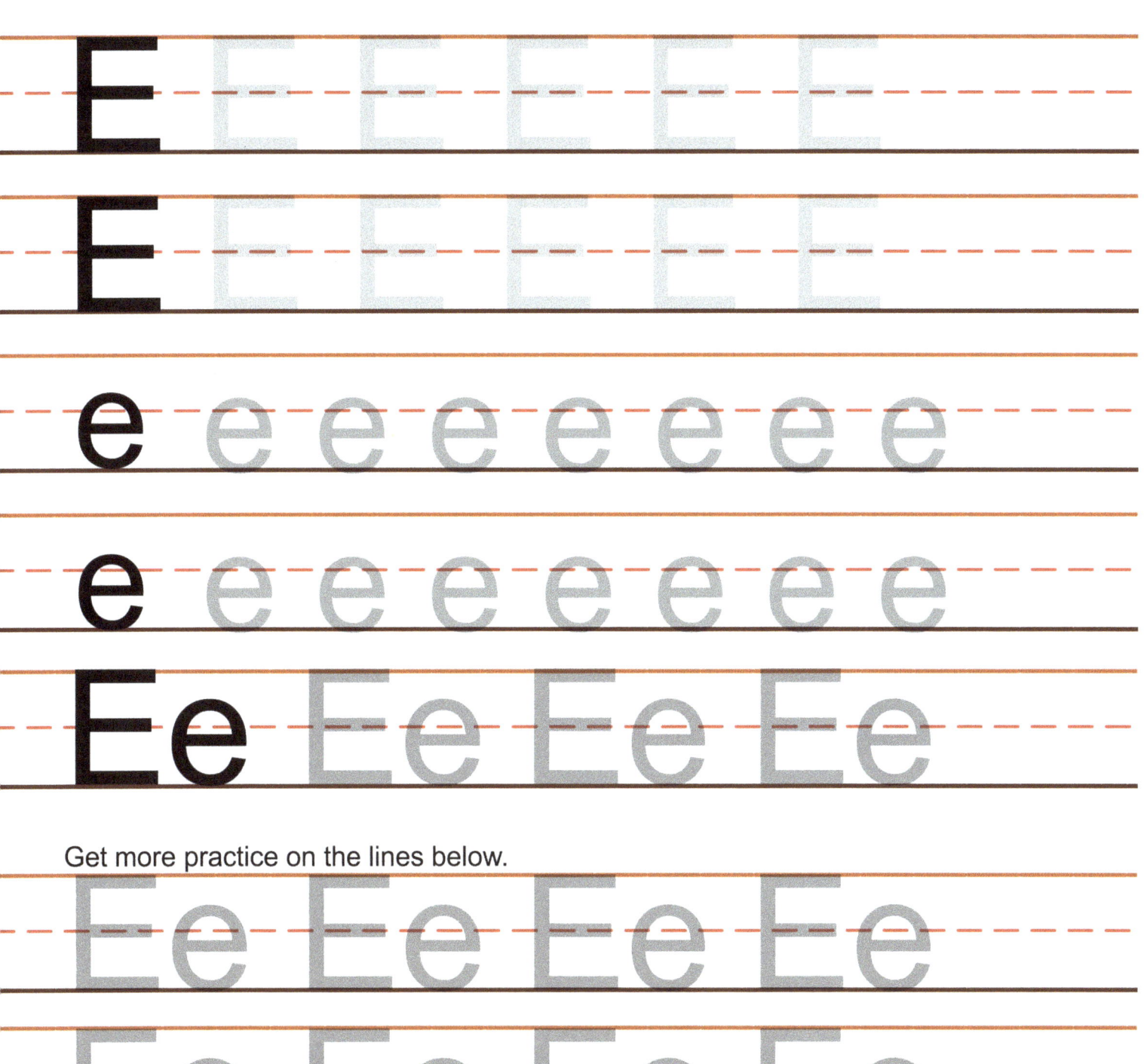

Get more practice on the lines below.

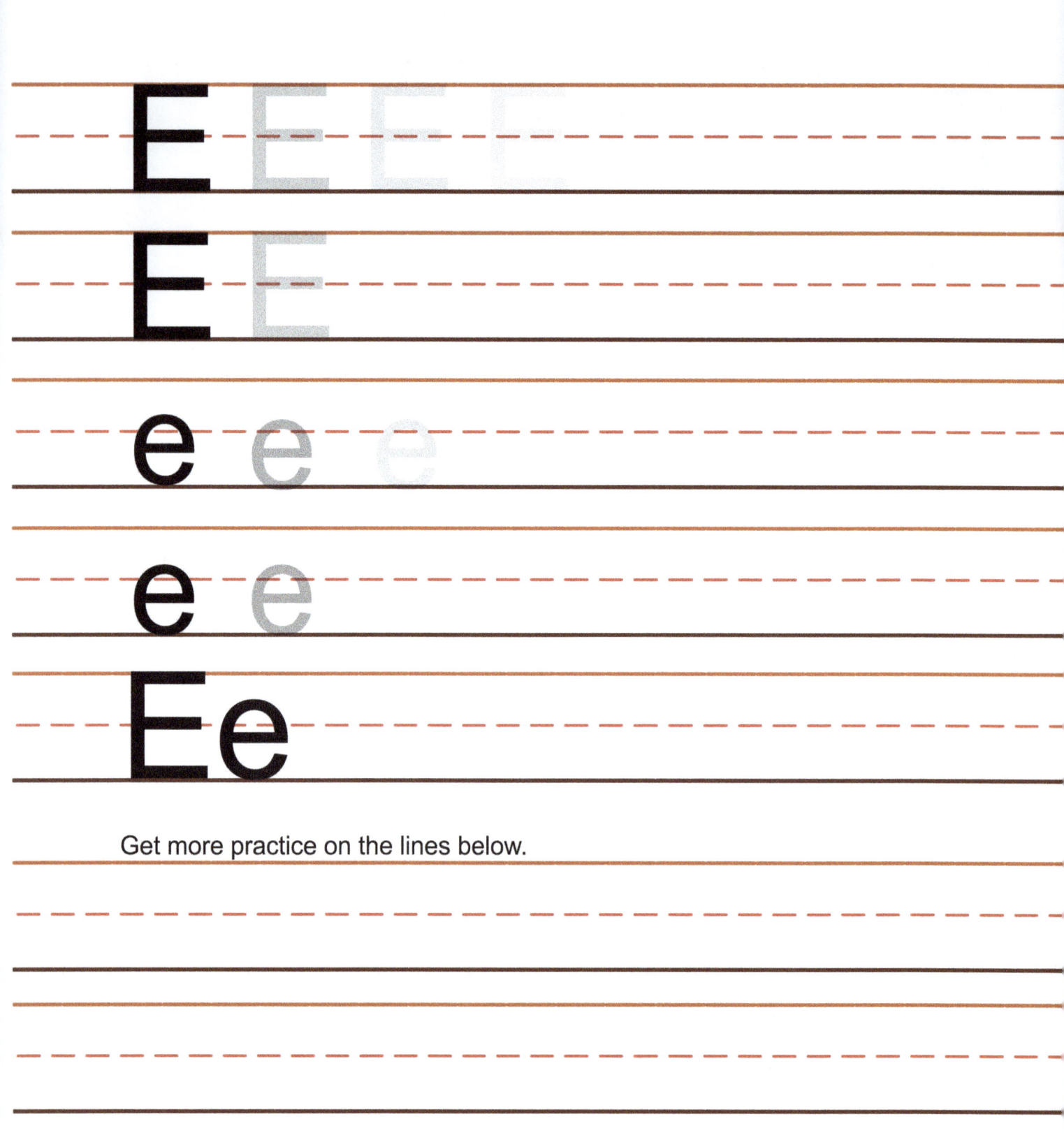

Get more practice on the lines below.

Get more practice on the lines below.

Color the letters.

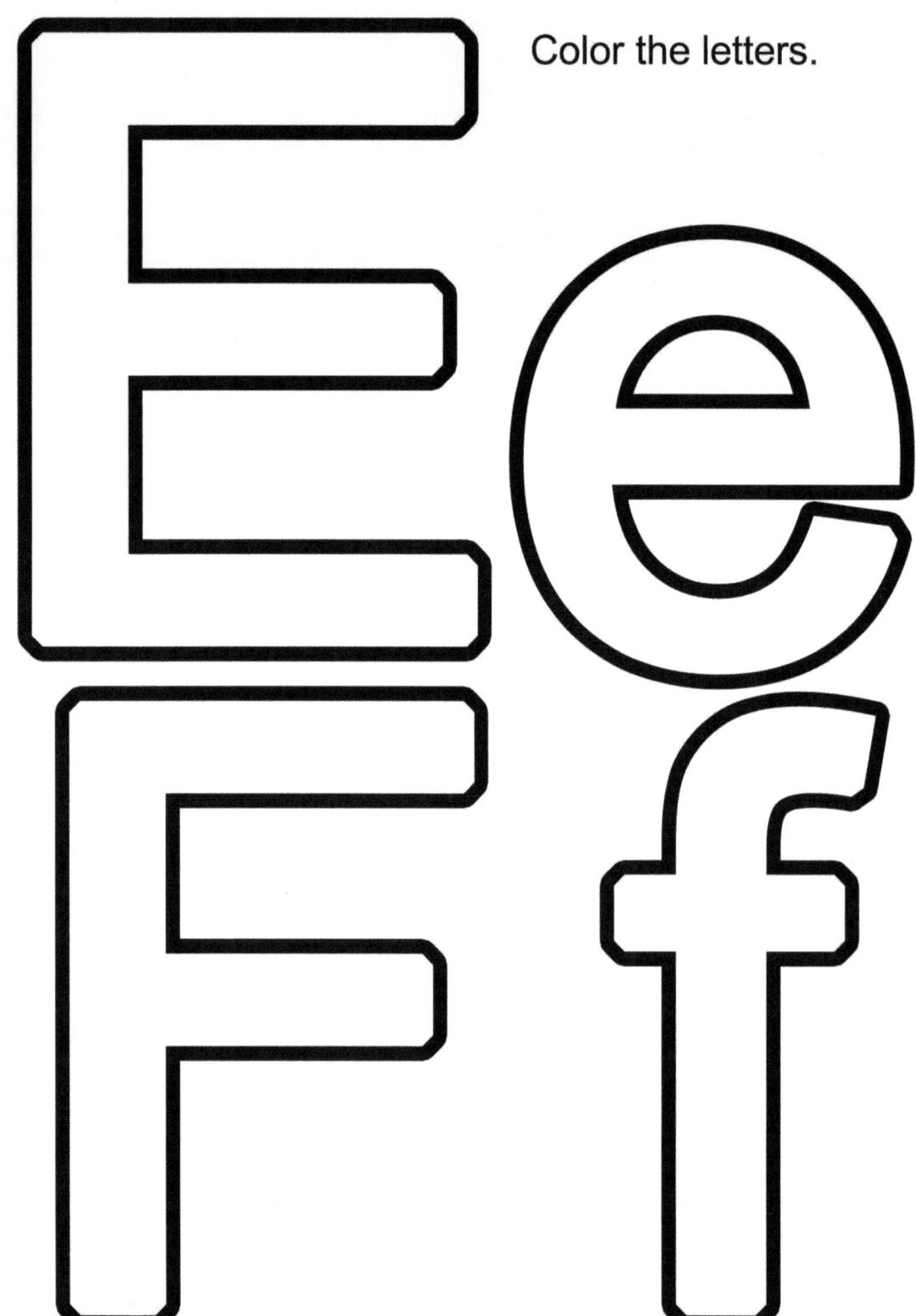

Get more practice on the lines below.

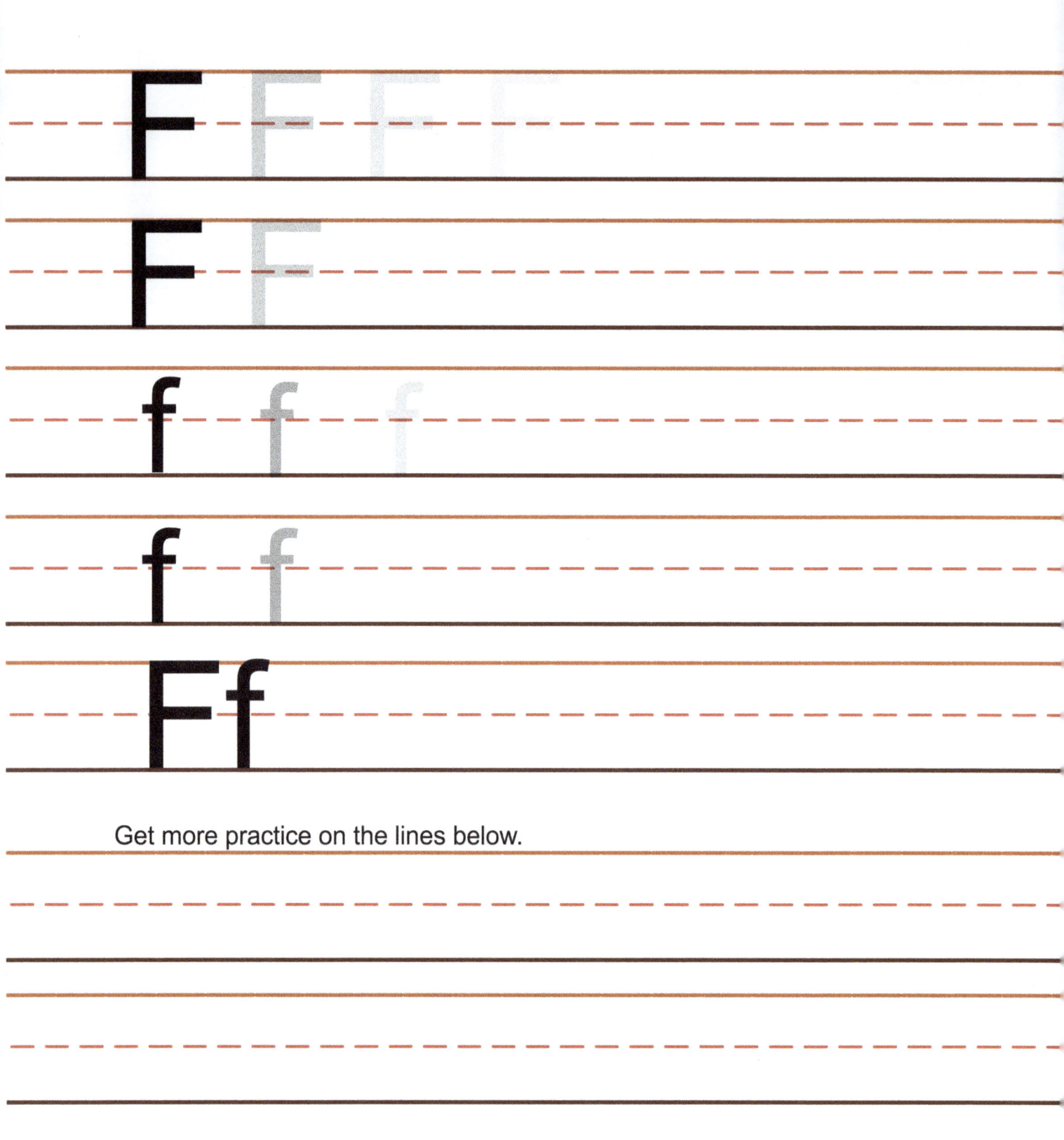

Get more practice on the lines below.

Get more practice on the lines below.

Color the letters.

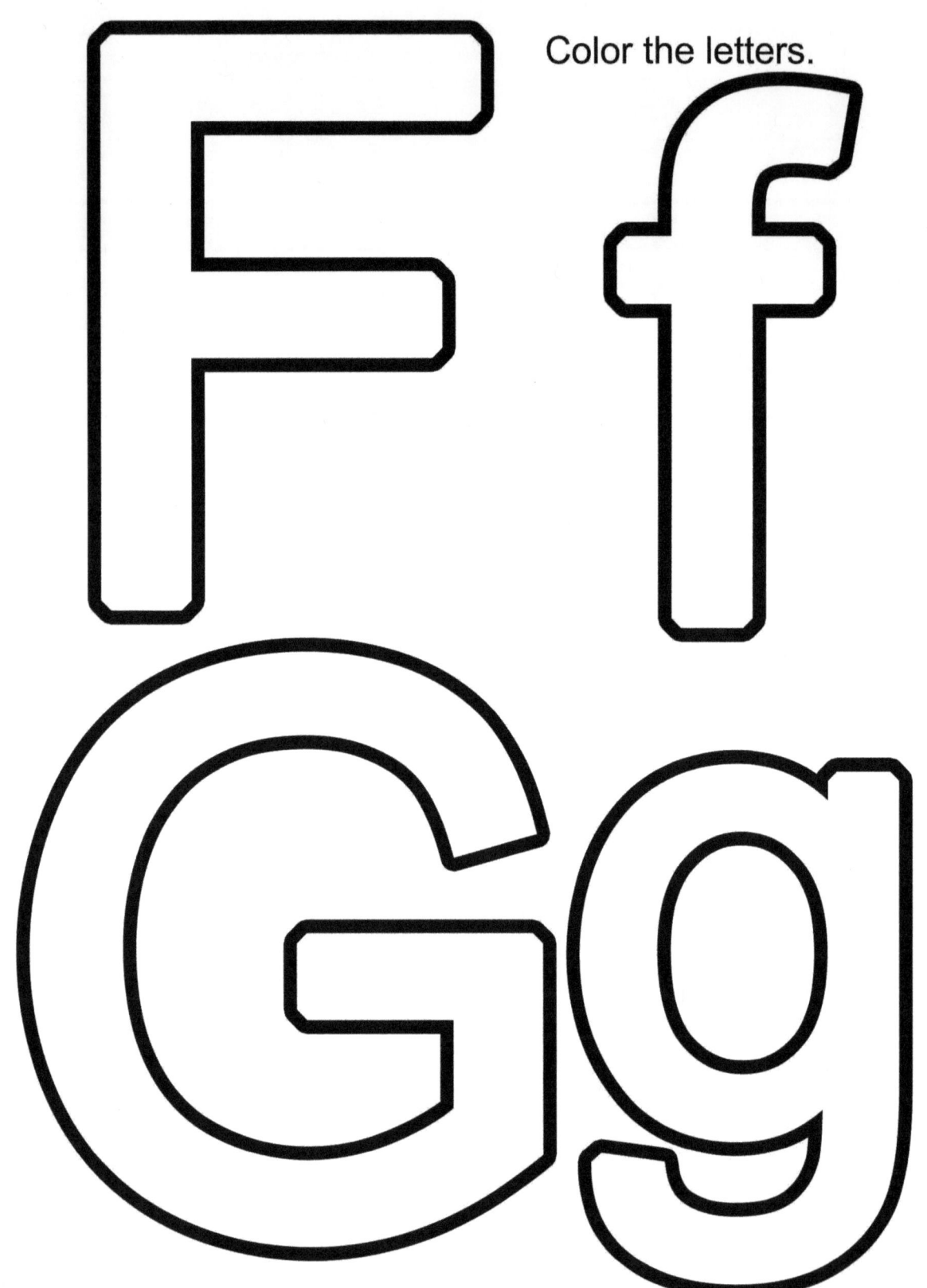

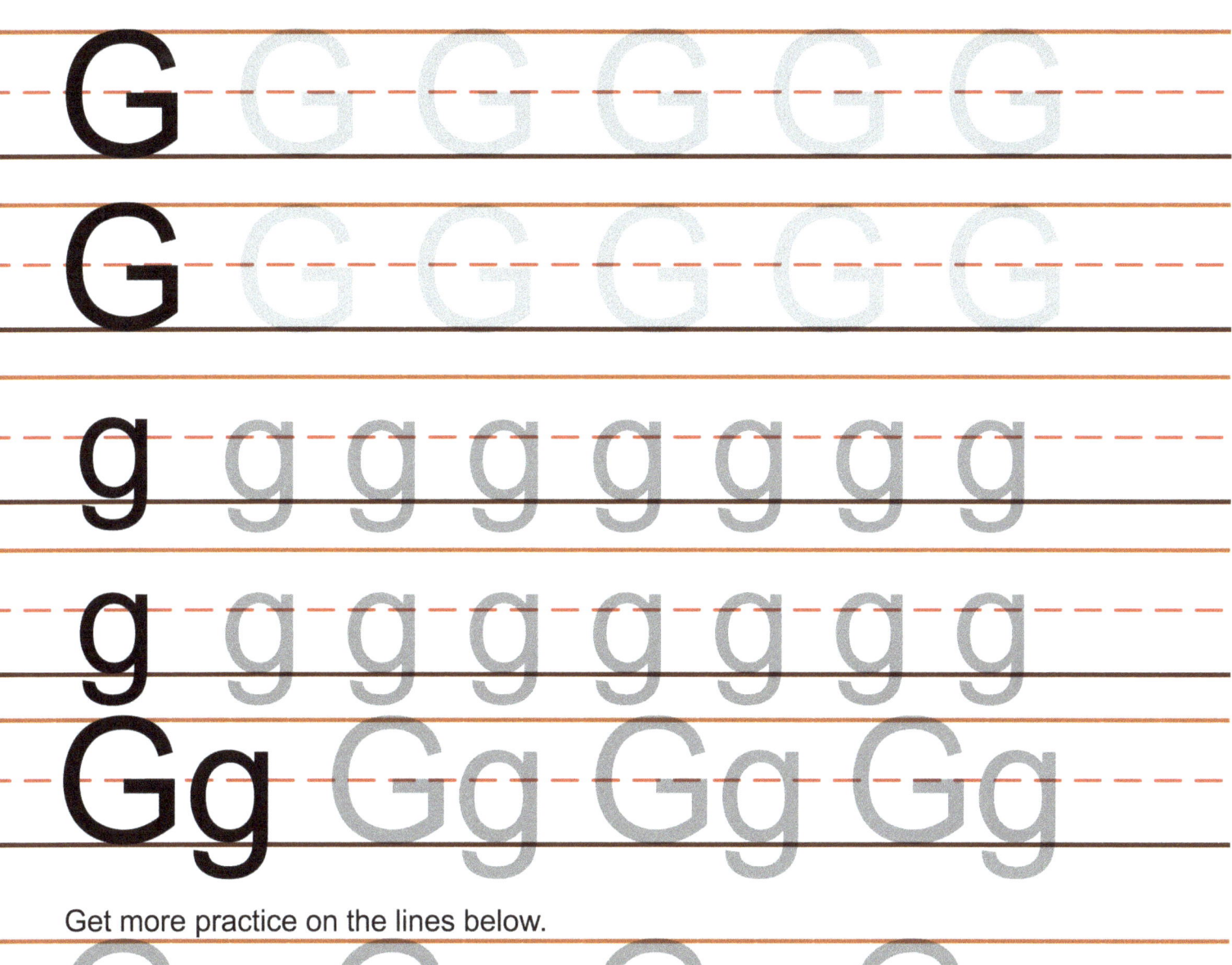

Get more practice on the lines below.

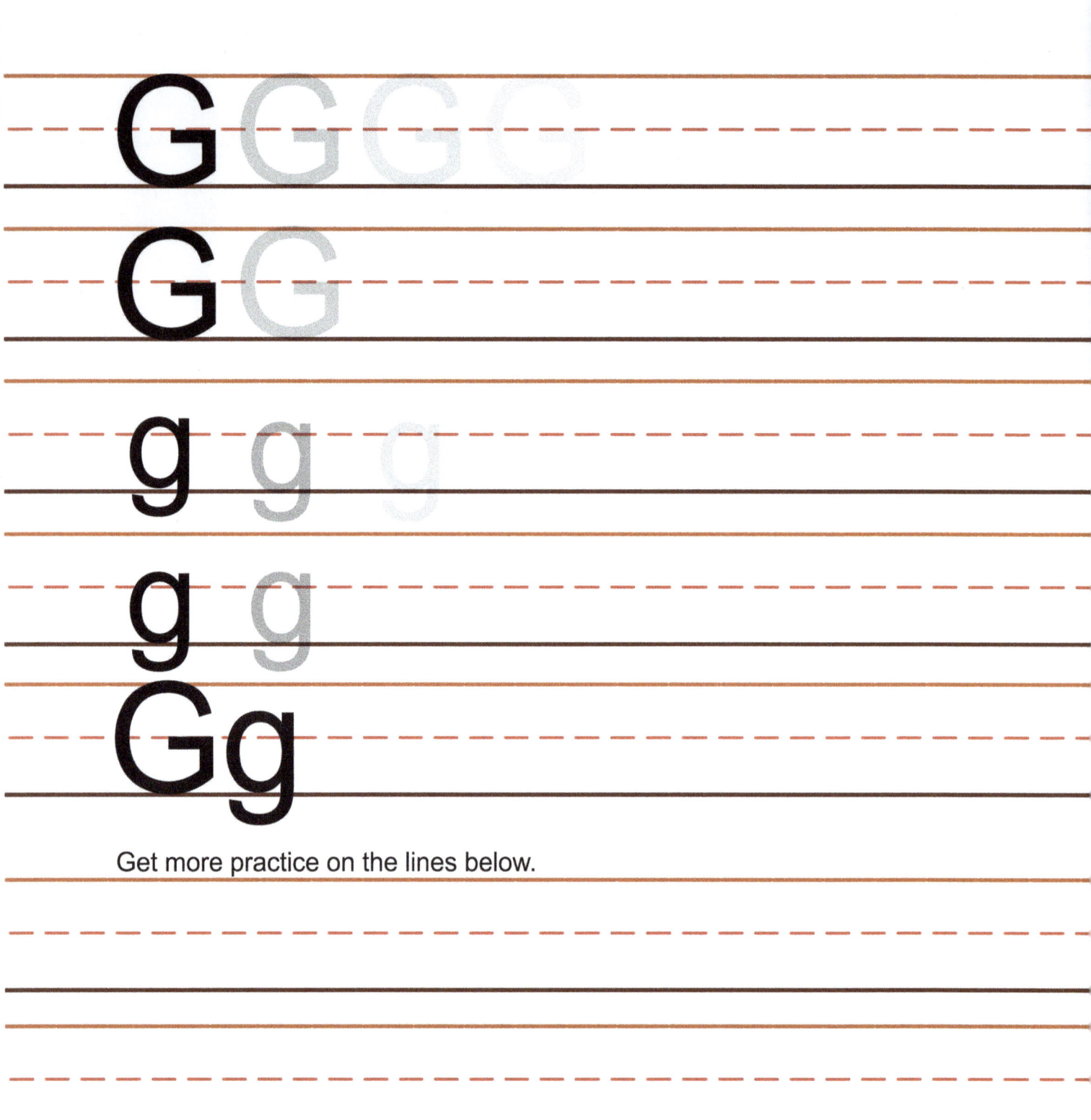

Get more practice on the lines below.

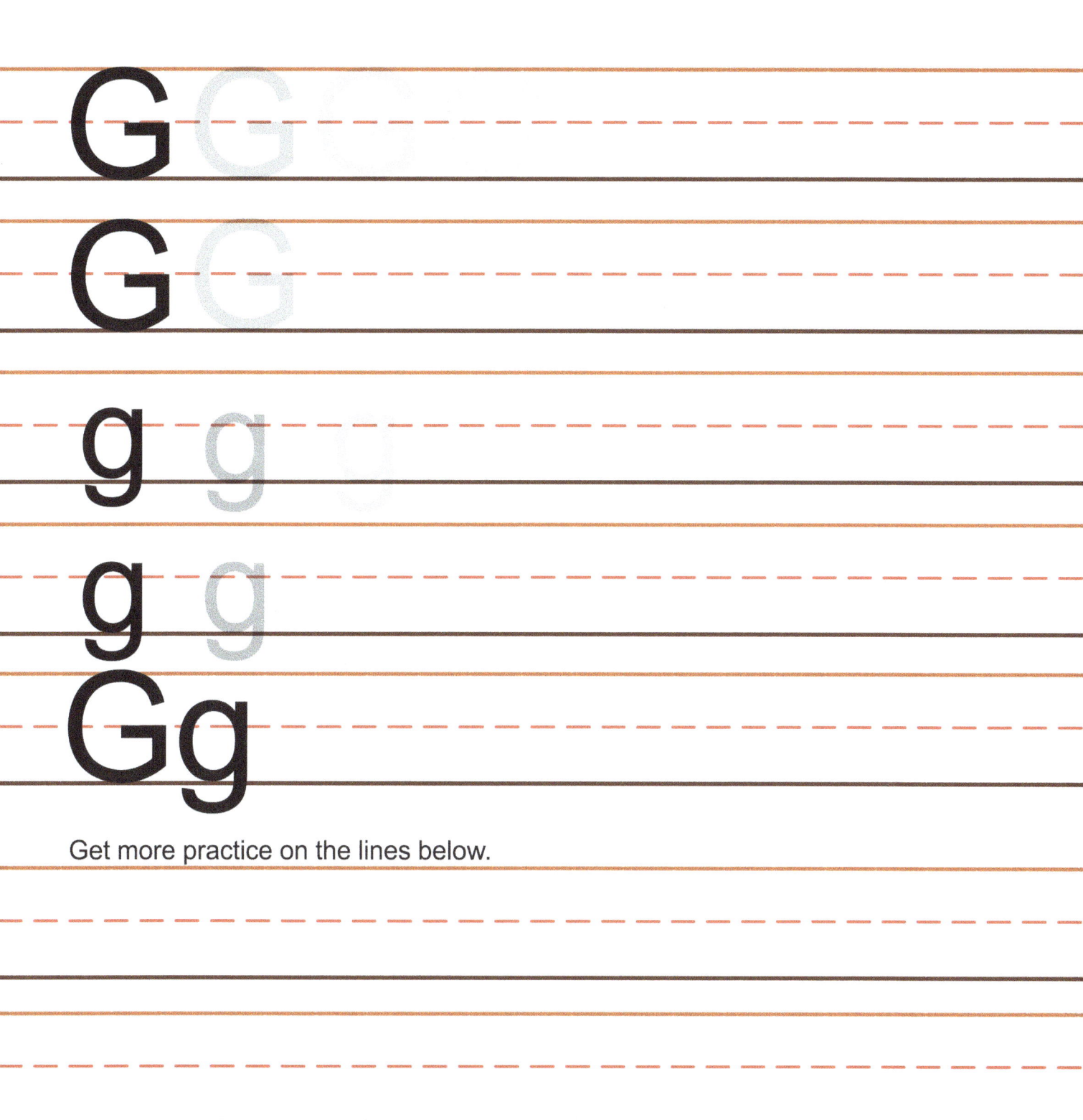

Color the letters.

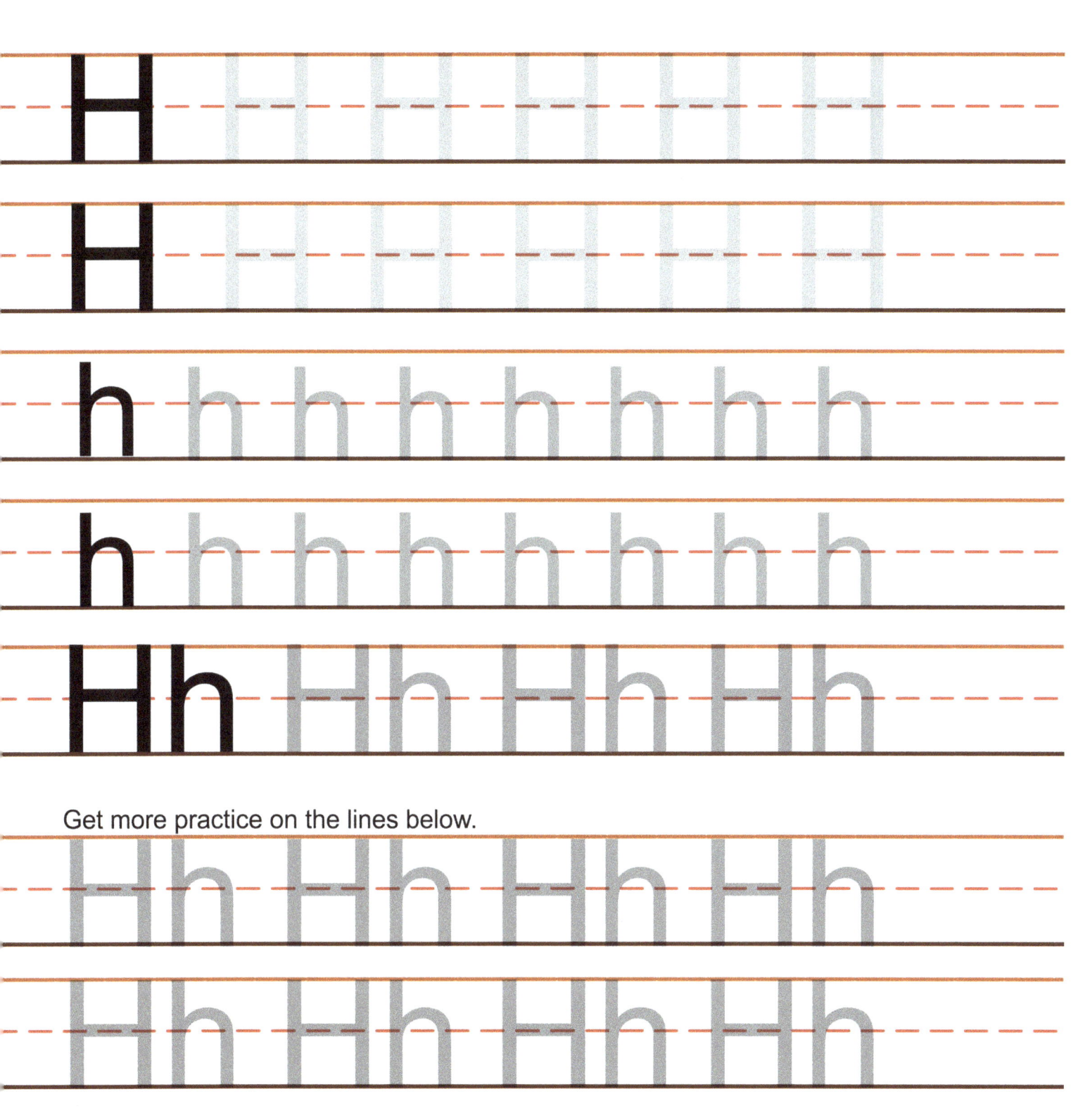
Get more practice on the lines below.

Get more practice on the lines below.

Get more practice on the lines below.

Color the letters.

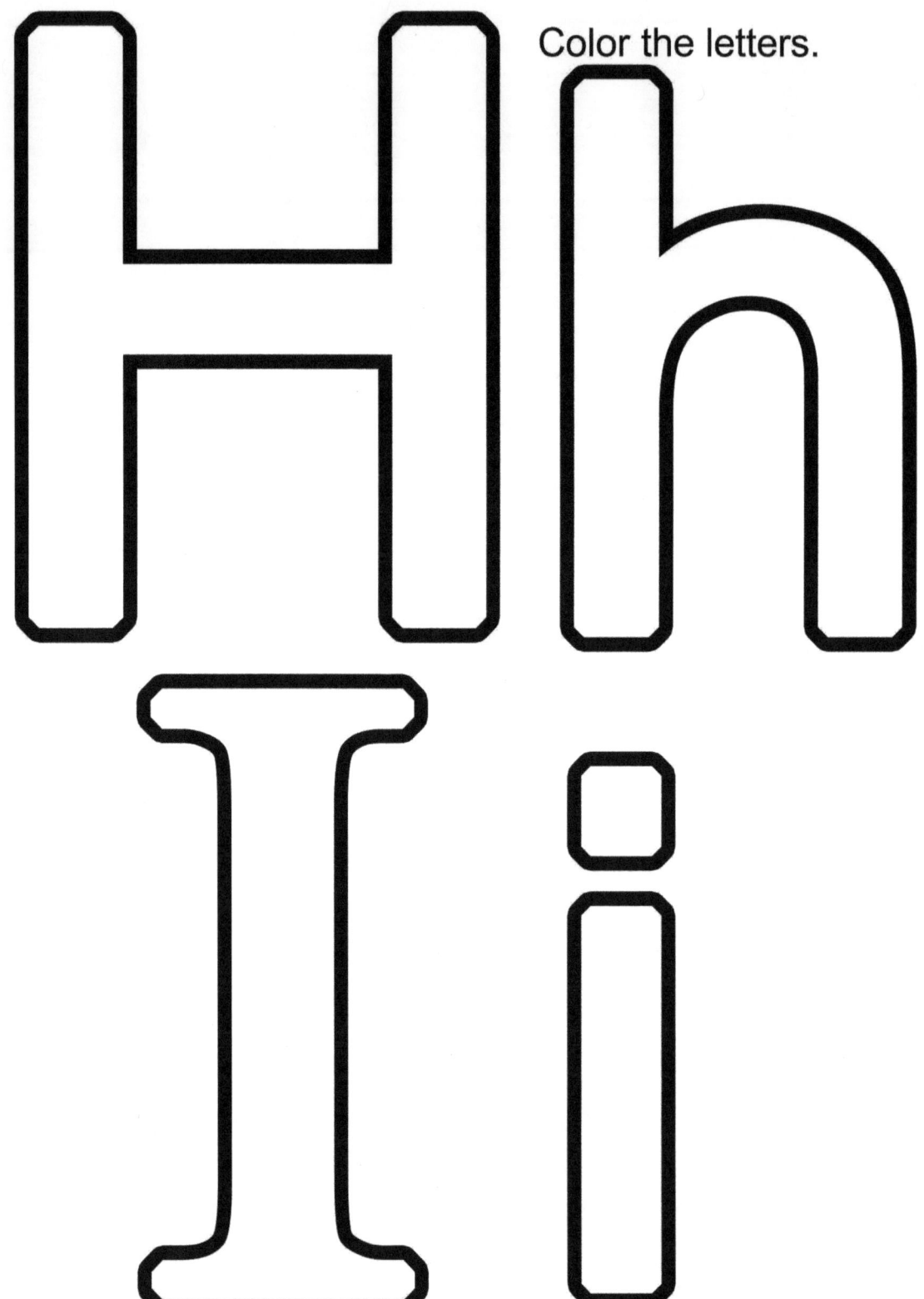

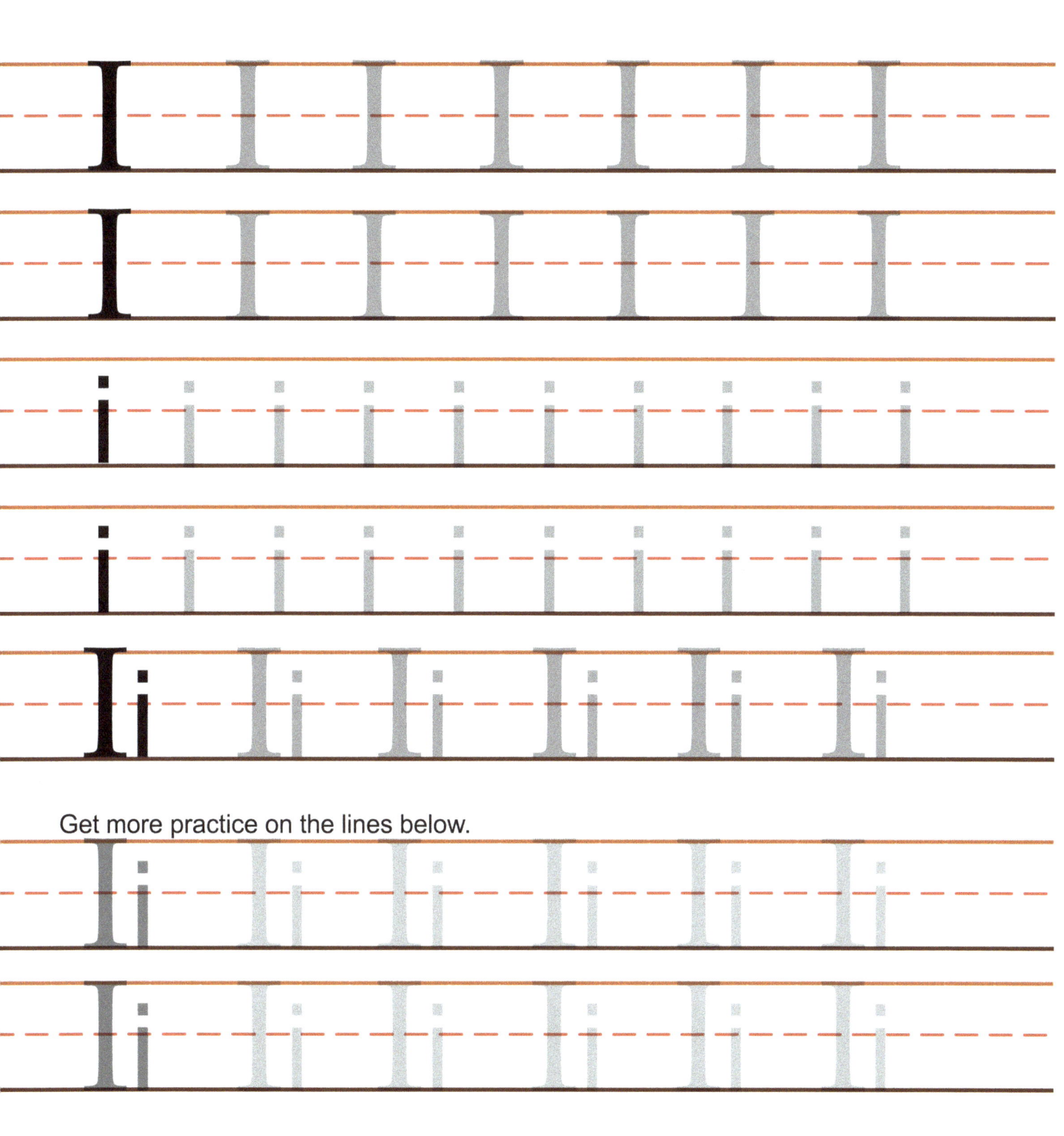
Get more practice on the lines below.

Get more practice on the lines below.

Get more practice on the lines below.

Color the letters.

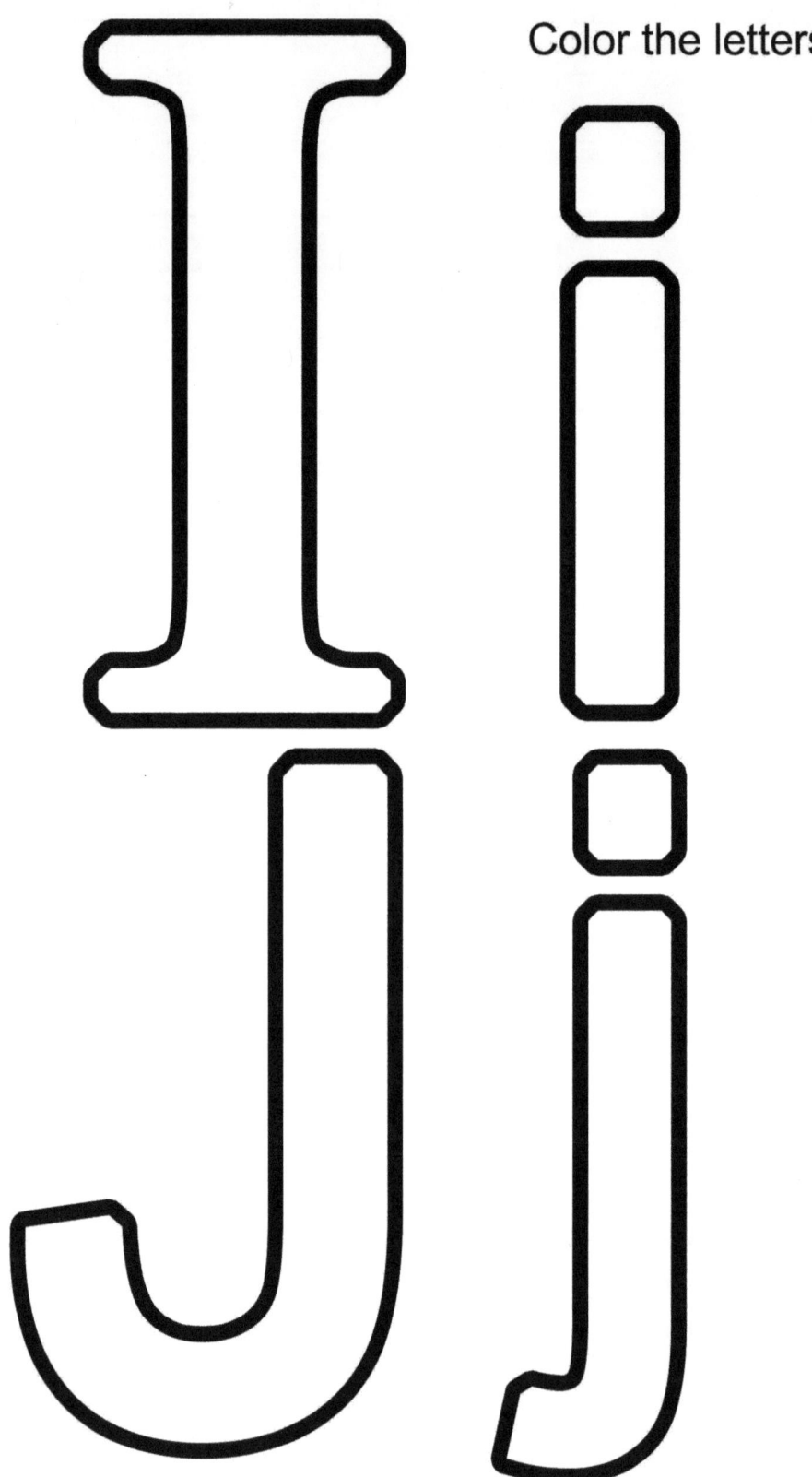

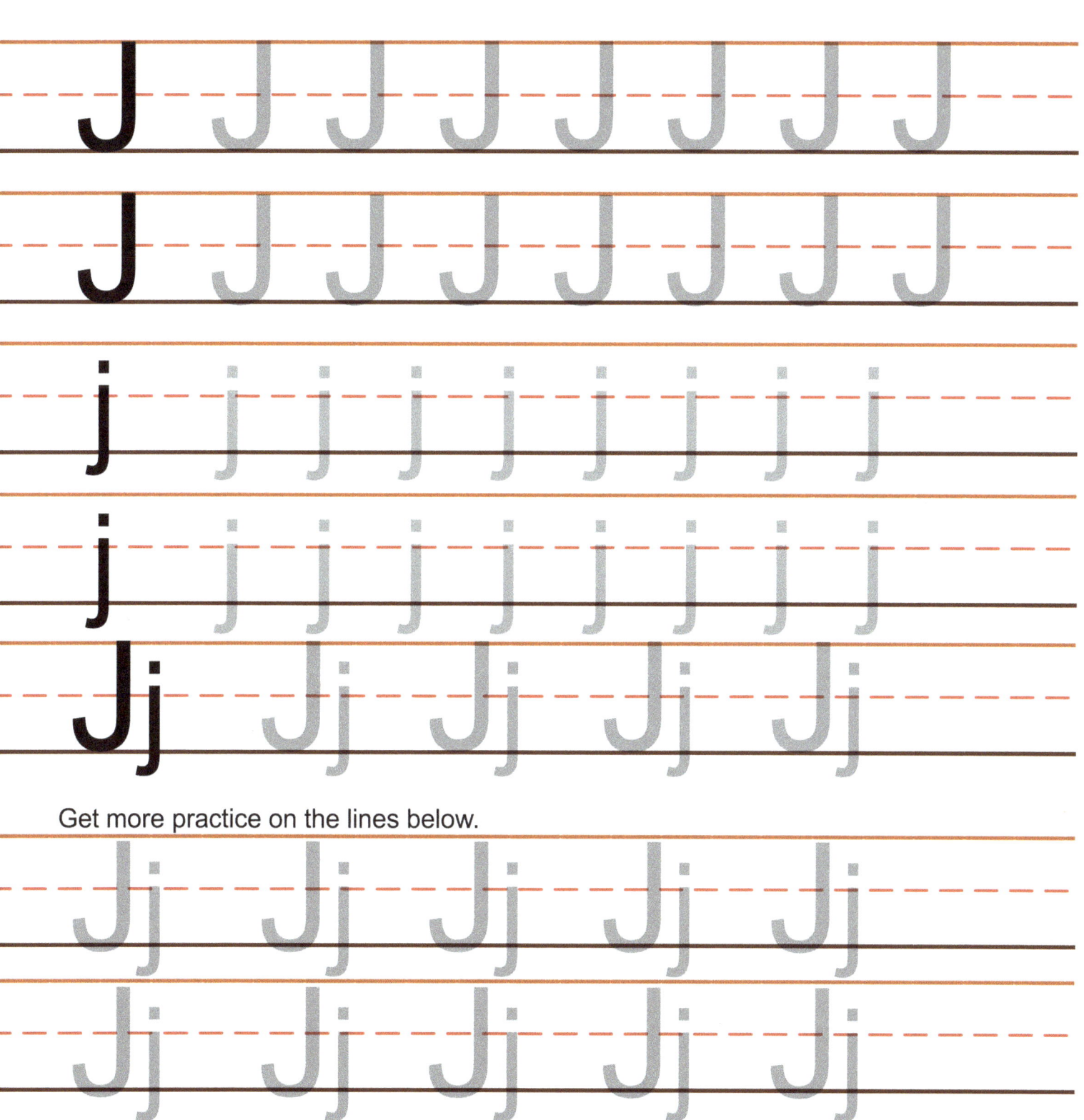

Get more practice on the lines below.

Get more practice on the lines below.

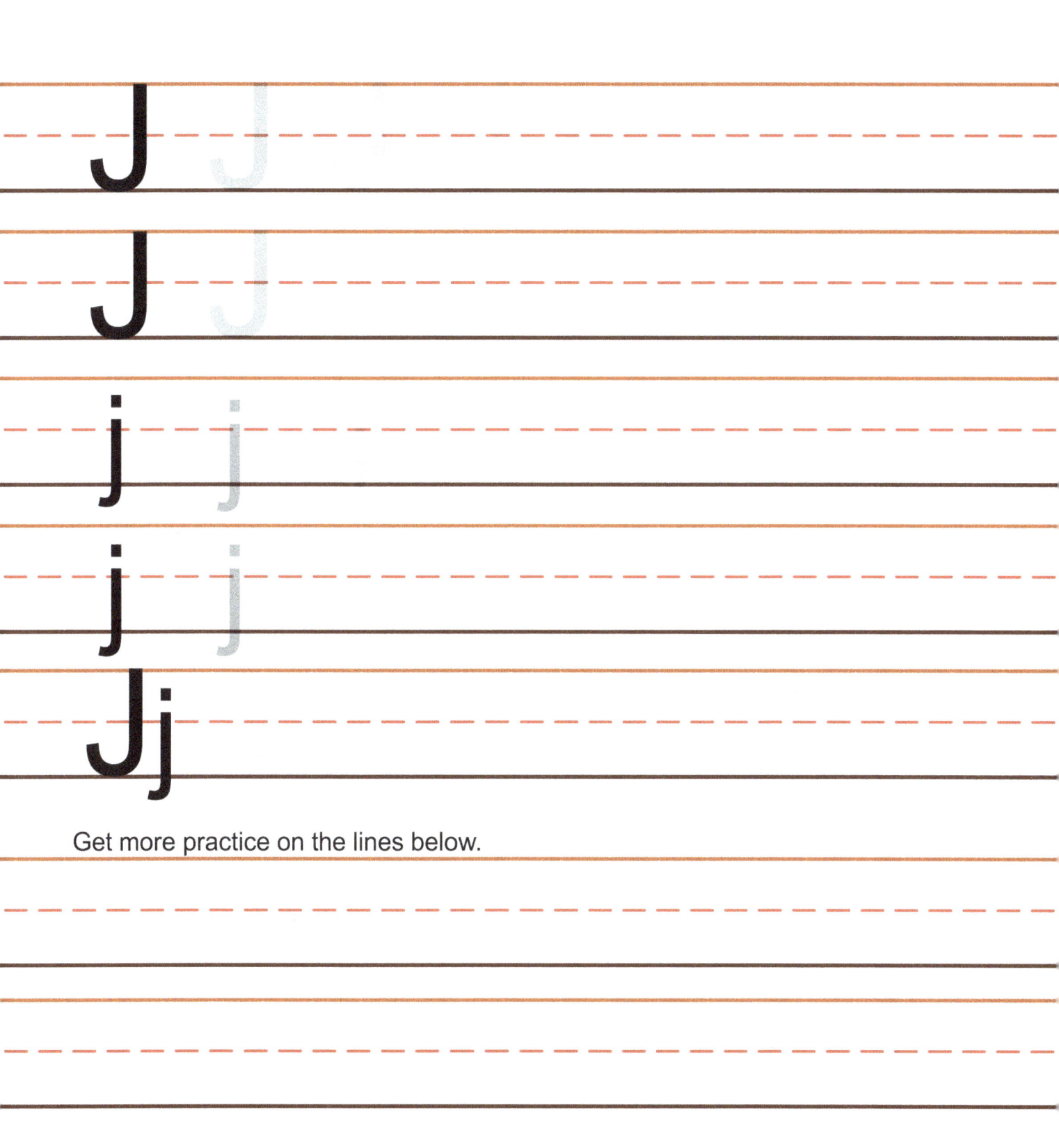

Get more practice on the lines below.

Color the letters.
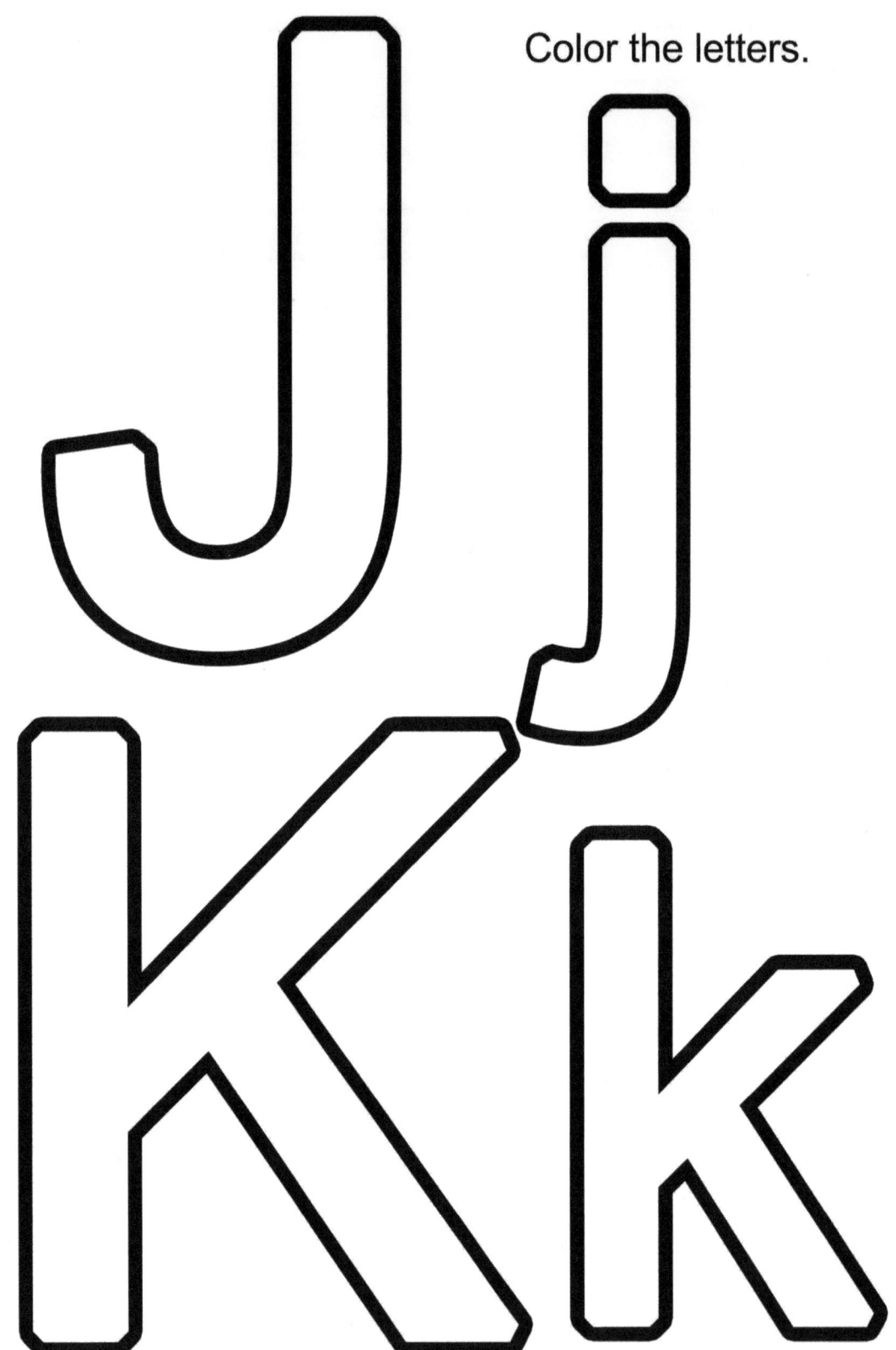

Get more practice on the lines below.

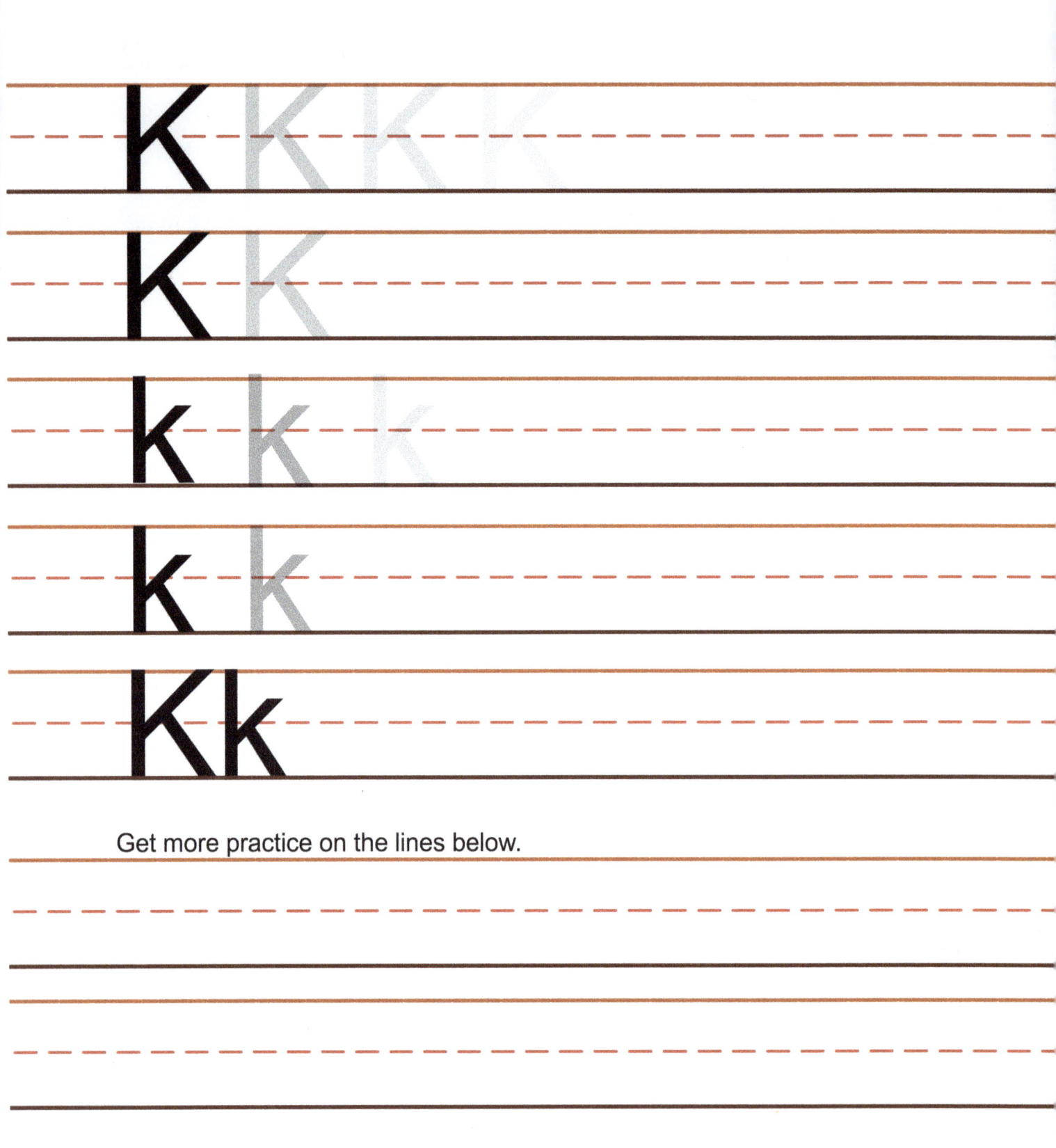

Get more practice on the lines below.

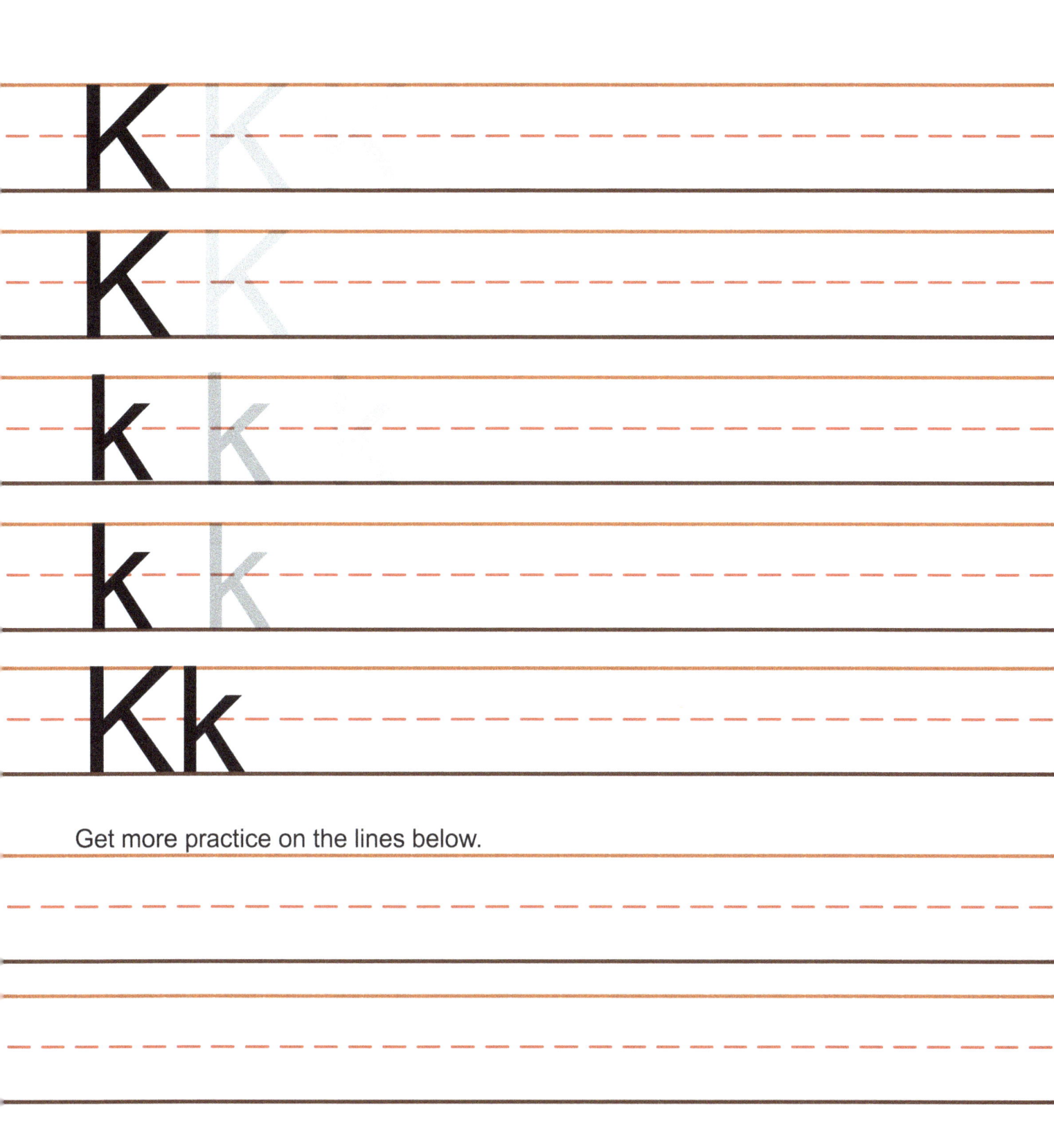

Get more practice on the lines below.

Color the letters.

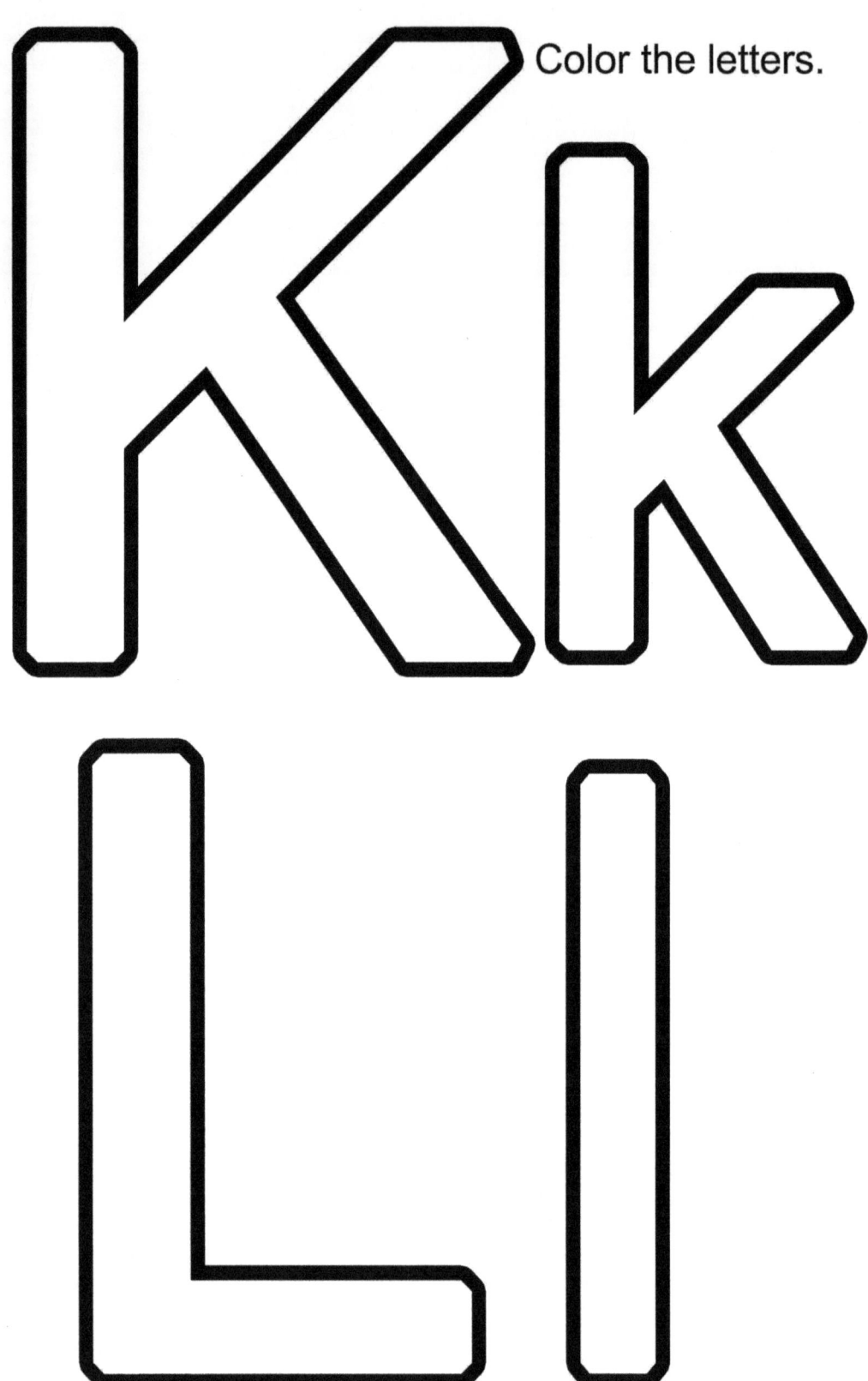

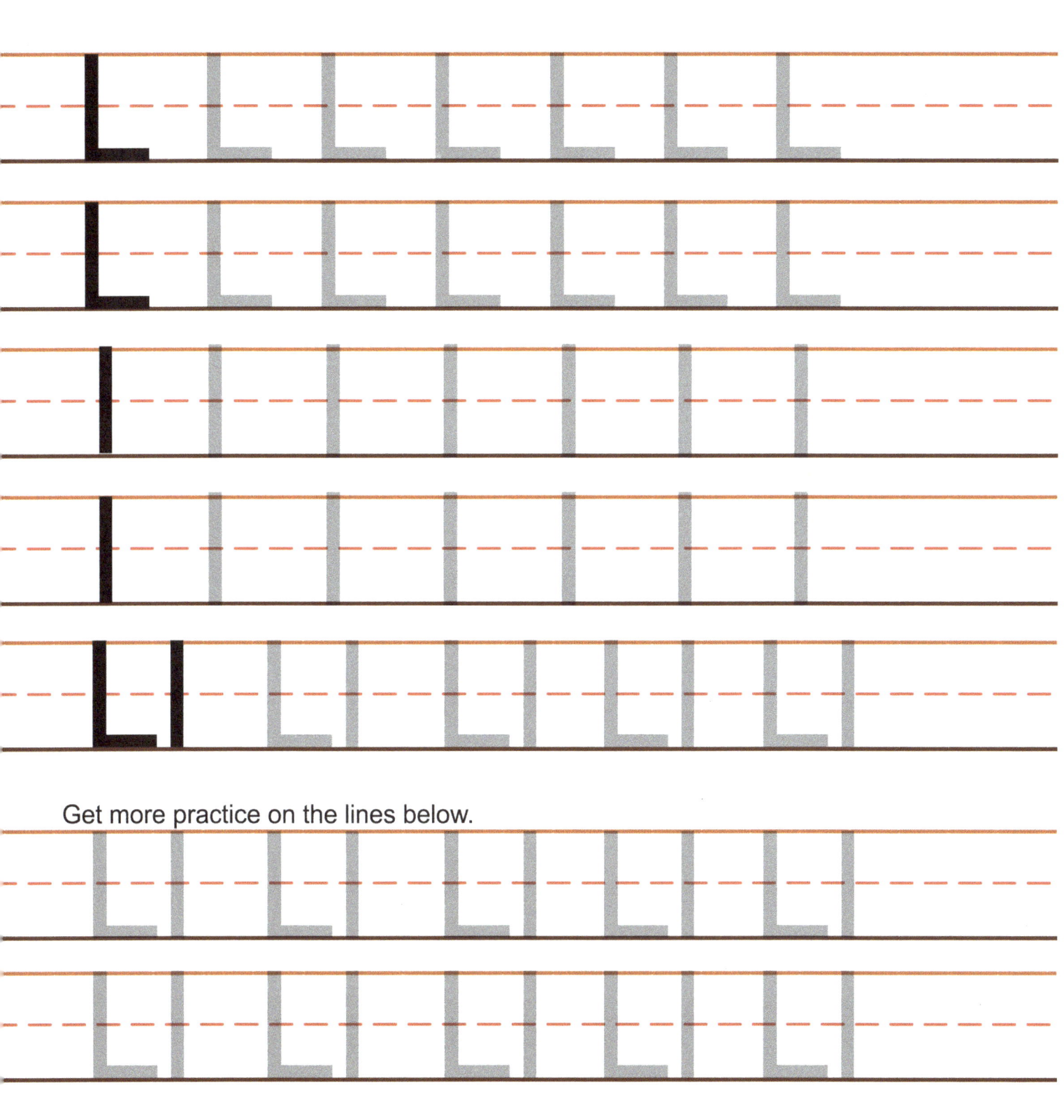
Get more practice on the lines below.

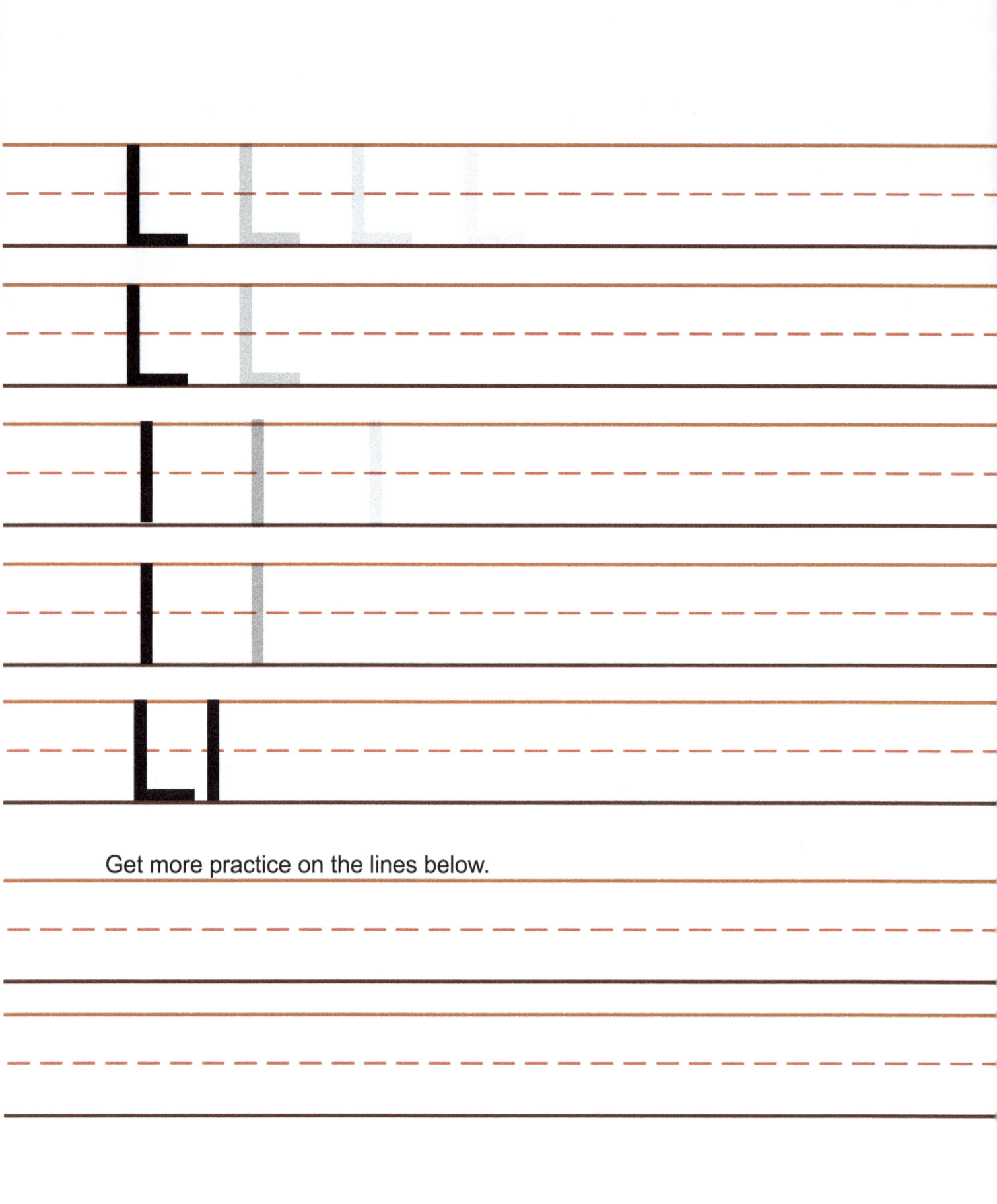

Get more practice on the lines below.

Get more practice on the lines below.

Color the letters.

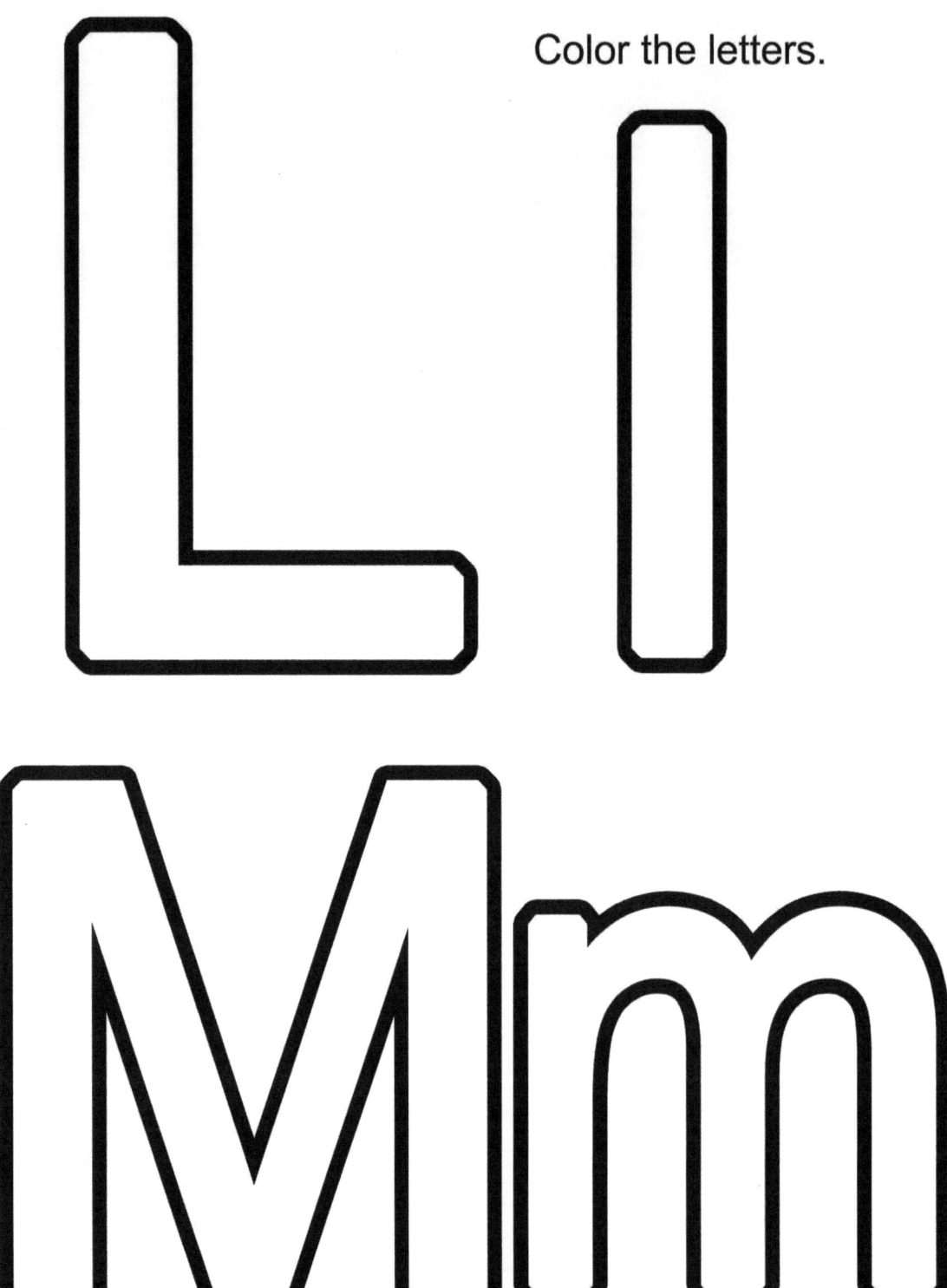

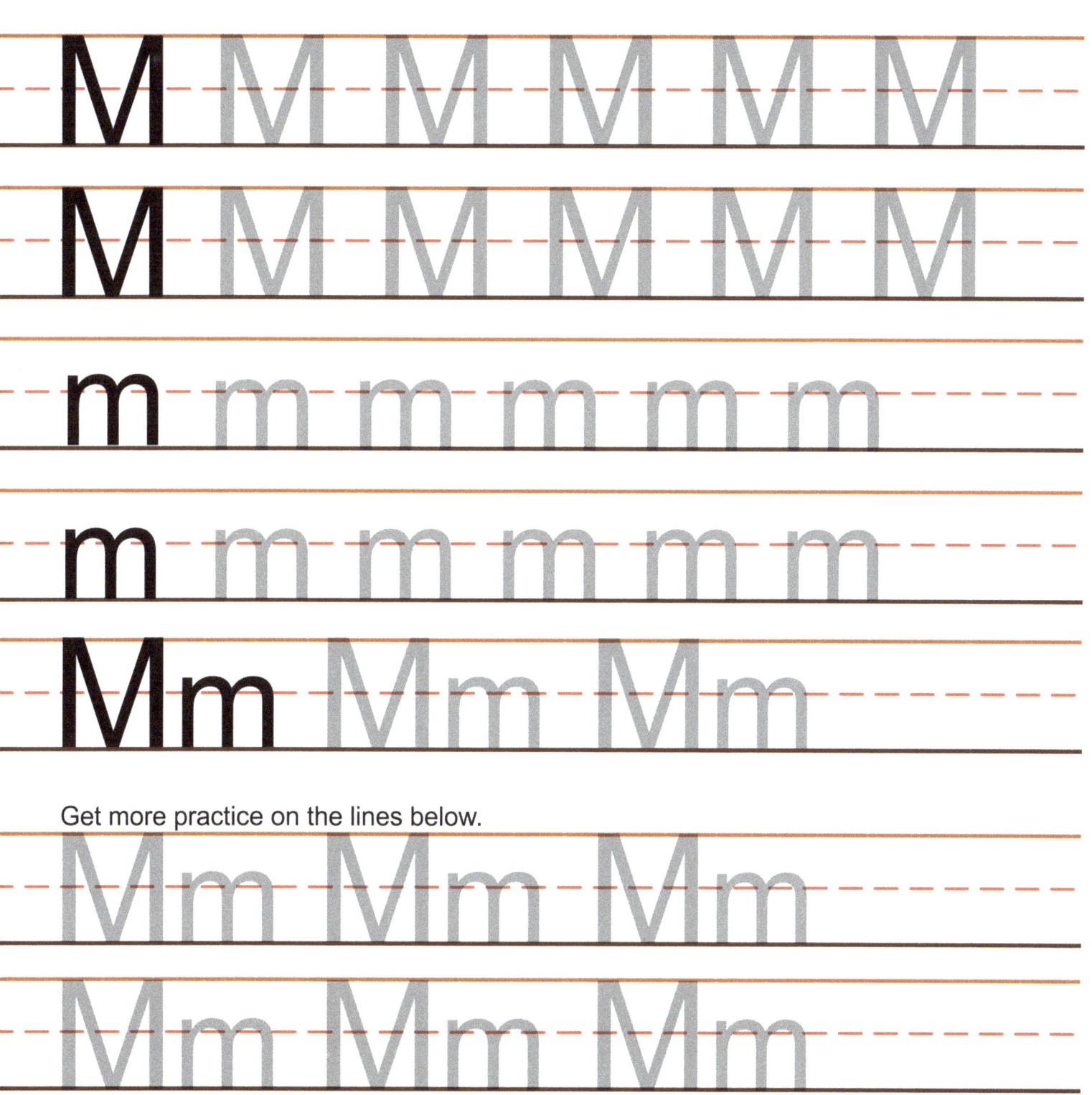

Get more practice on the lines below.

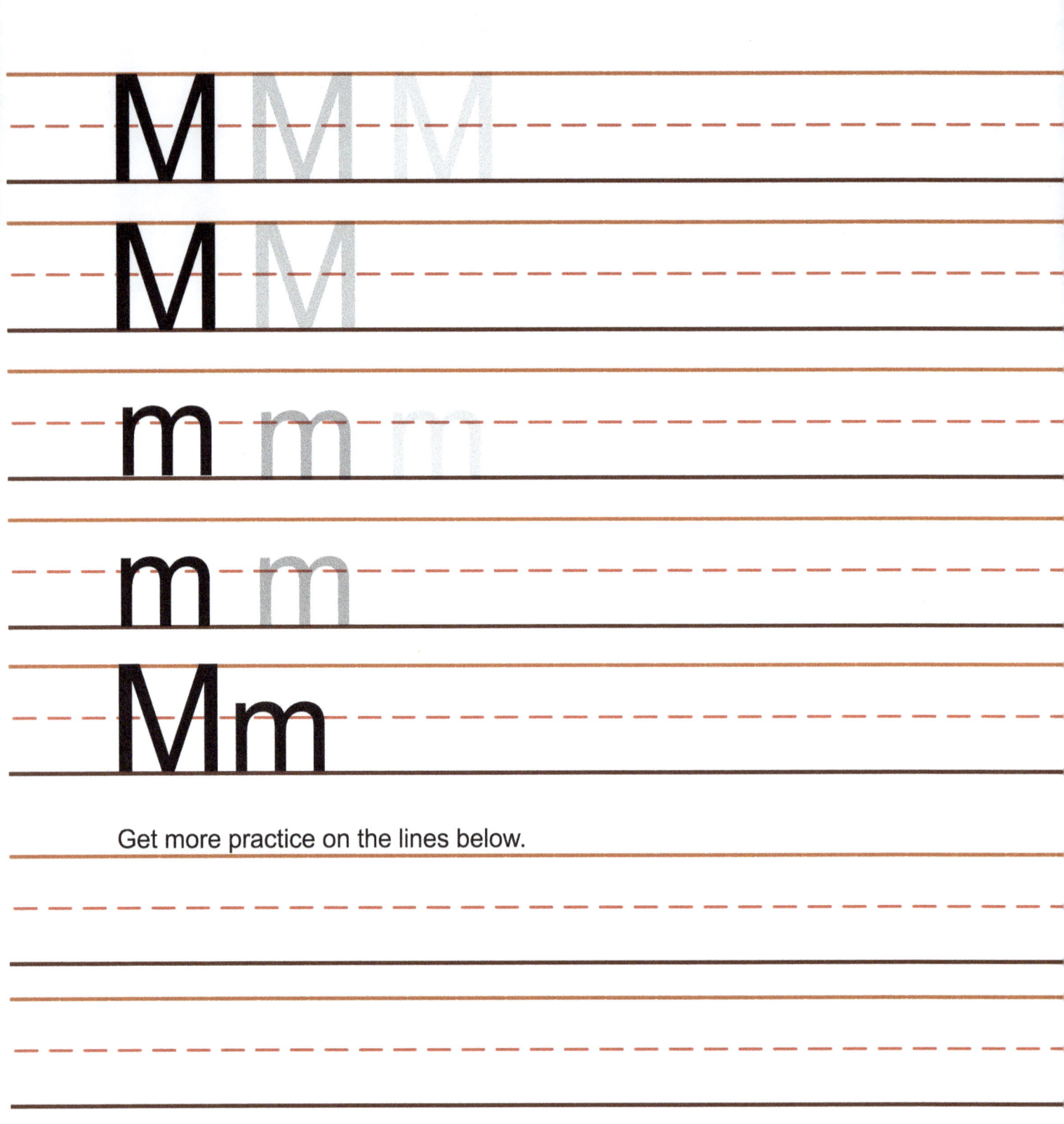

Get more practice on the lines below.

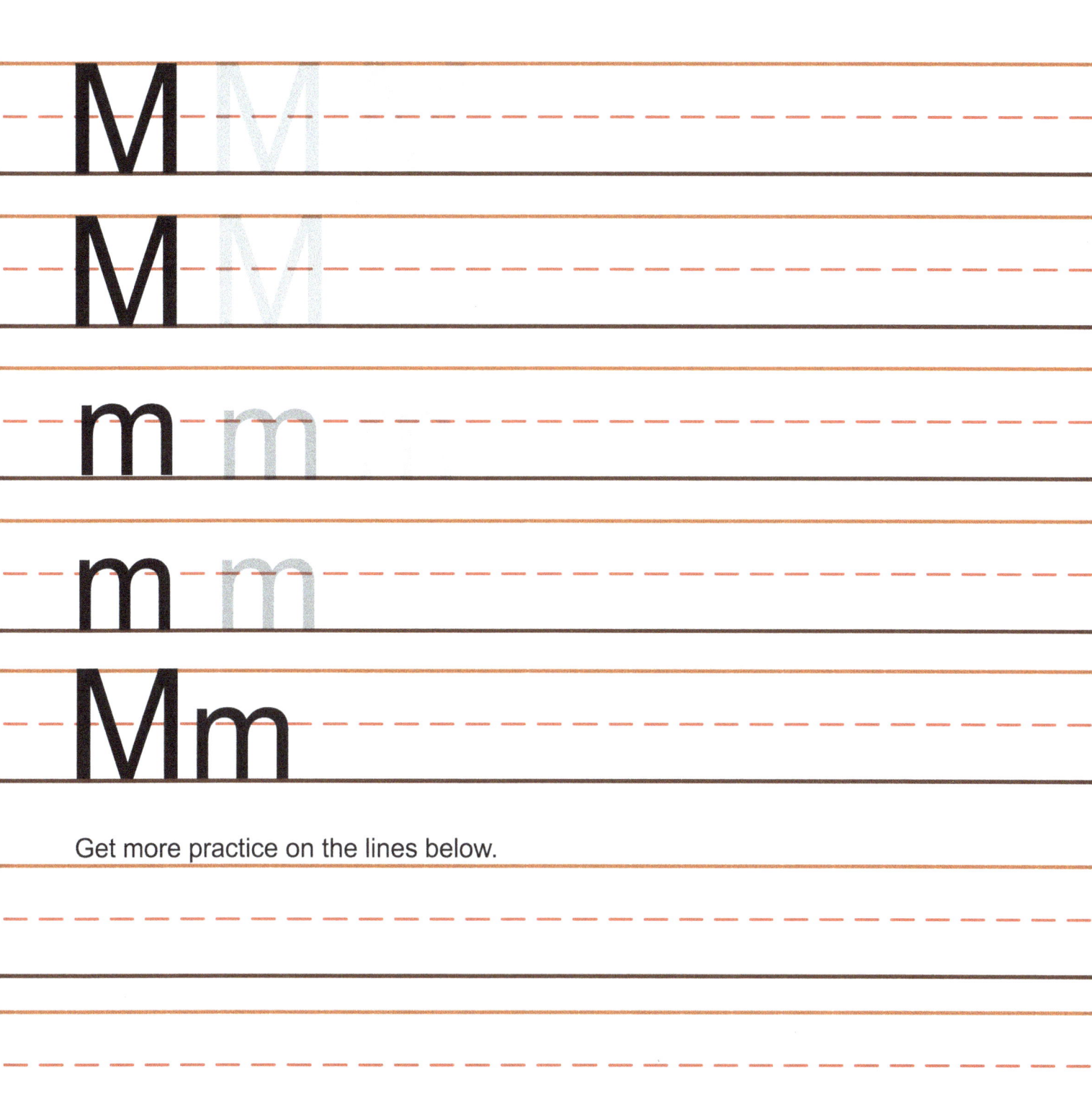

Get more practice on the lines below.

Color the letters.

Get more practice on the lines below.

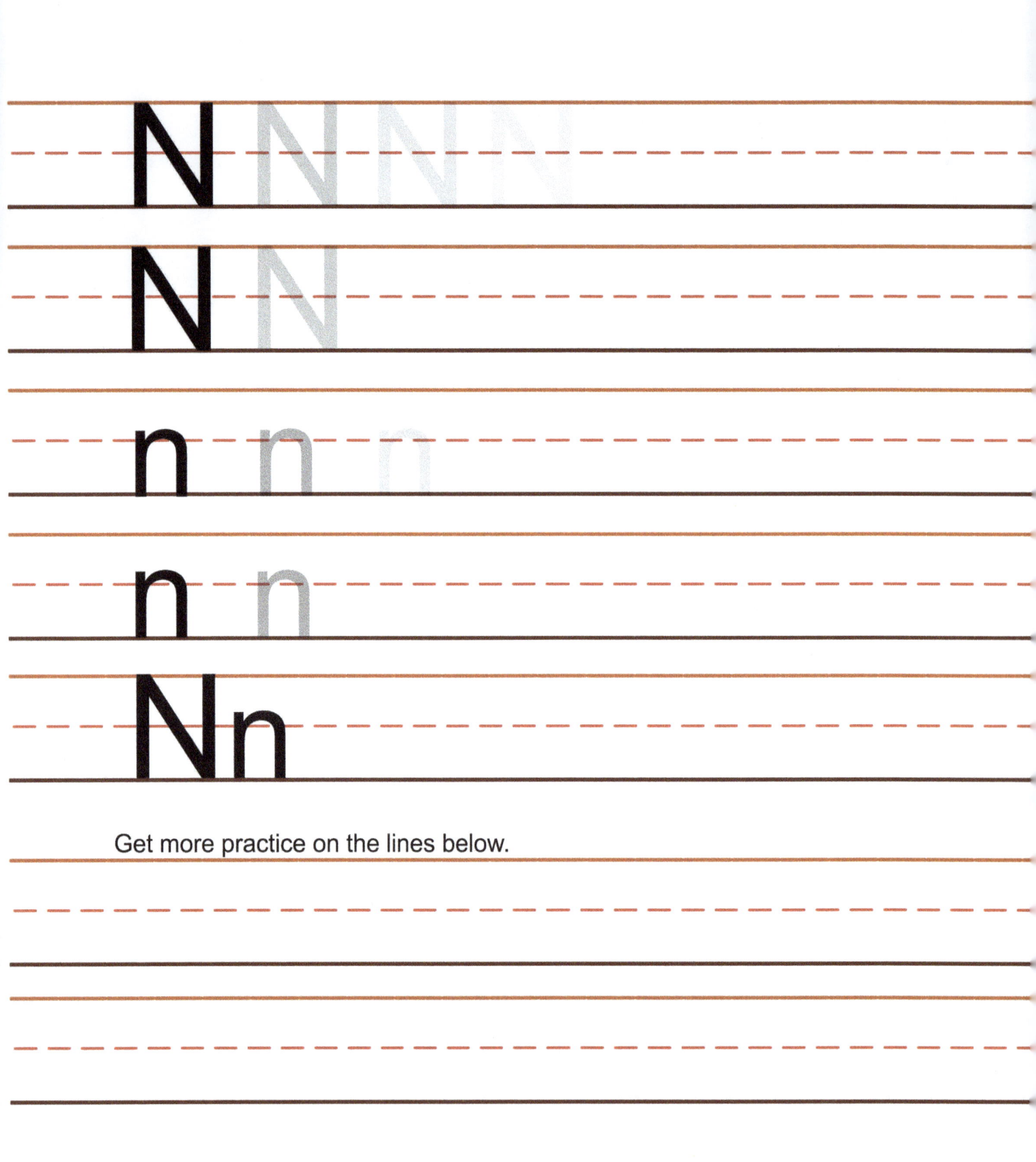

Get more practice on the lines below.

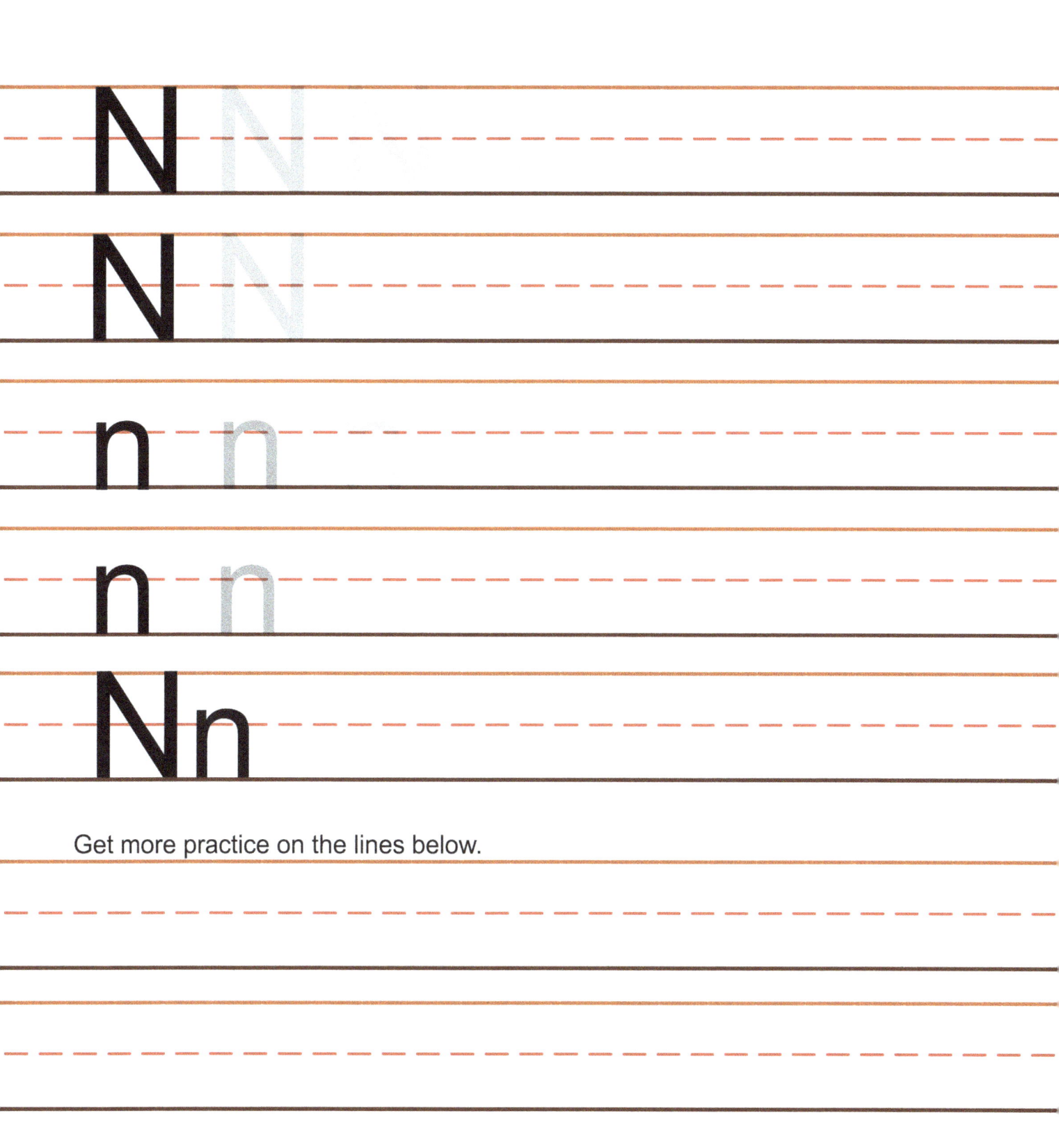

Get more practice on the lines below.

Color the letters.

Get more practice on the lines below.

Get more practice on the lines below.

Get more practice on the lines below.

Color the letters.

P P P P P P P

P P P P P P P

p p p p p p p

p p p p p p p

Pp Pp Pp Pp Pp

Get more practice on the lines below.

Pp Pp Pp Pp Pp

Pp Pp Pp Pp Pp

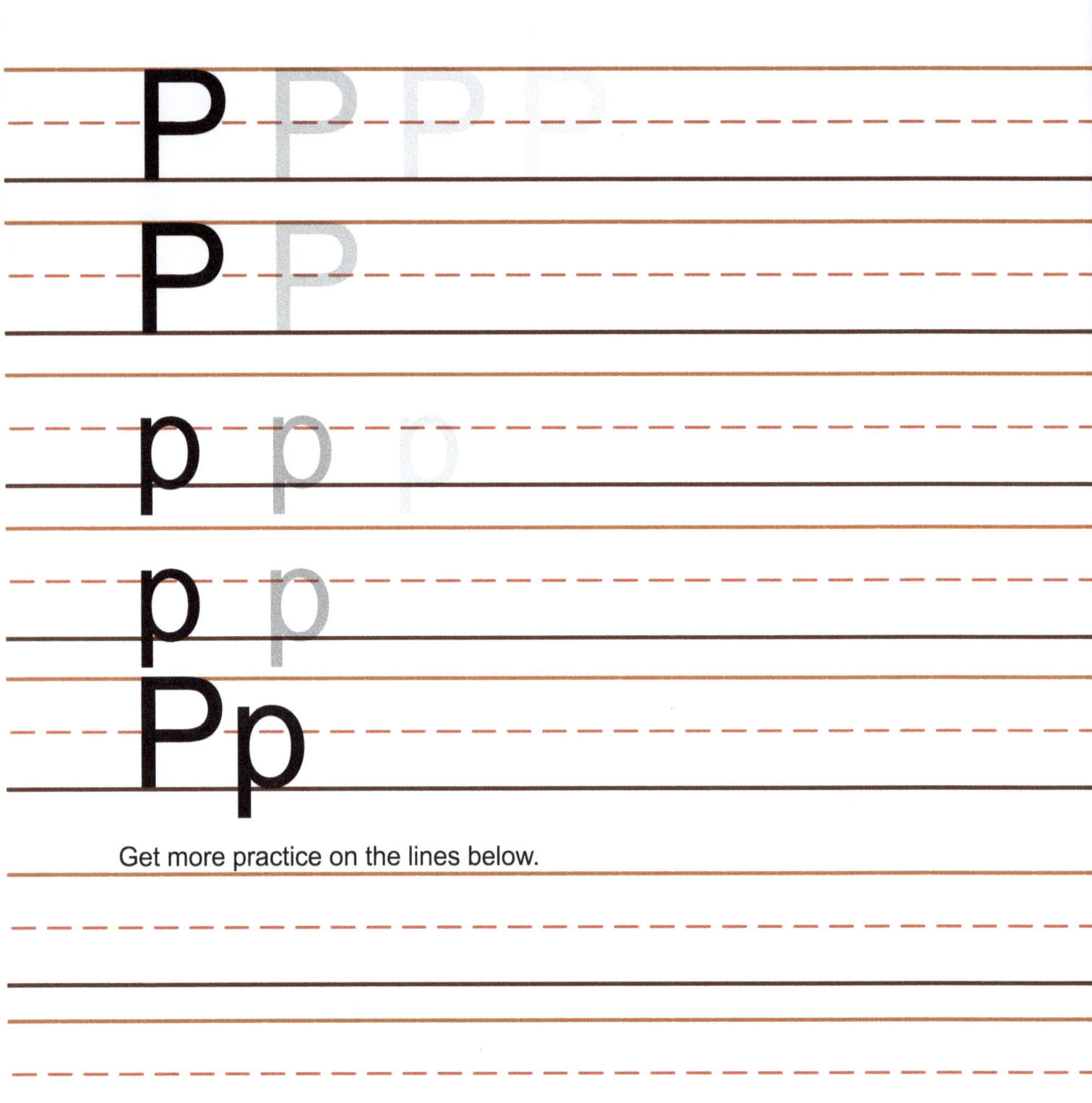

Get more practice on the lines below.

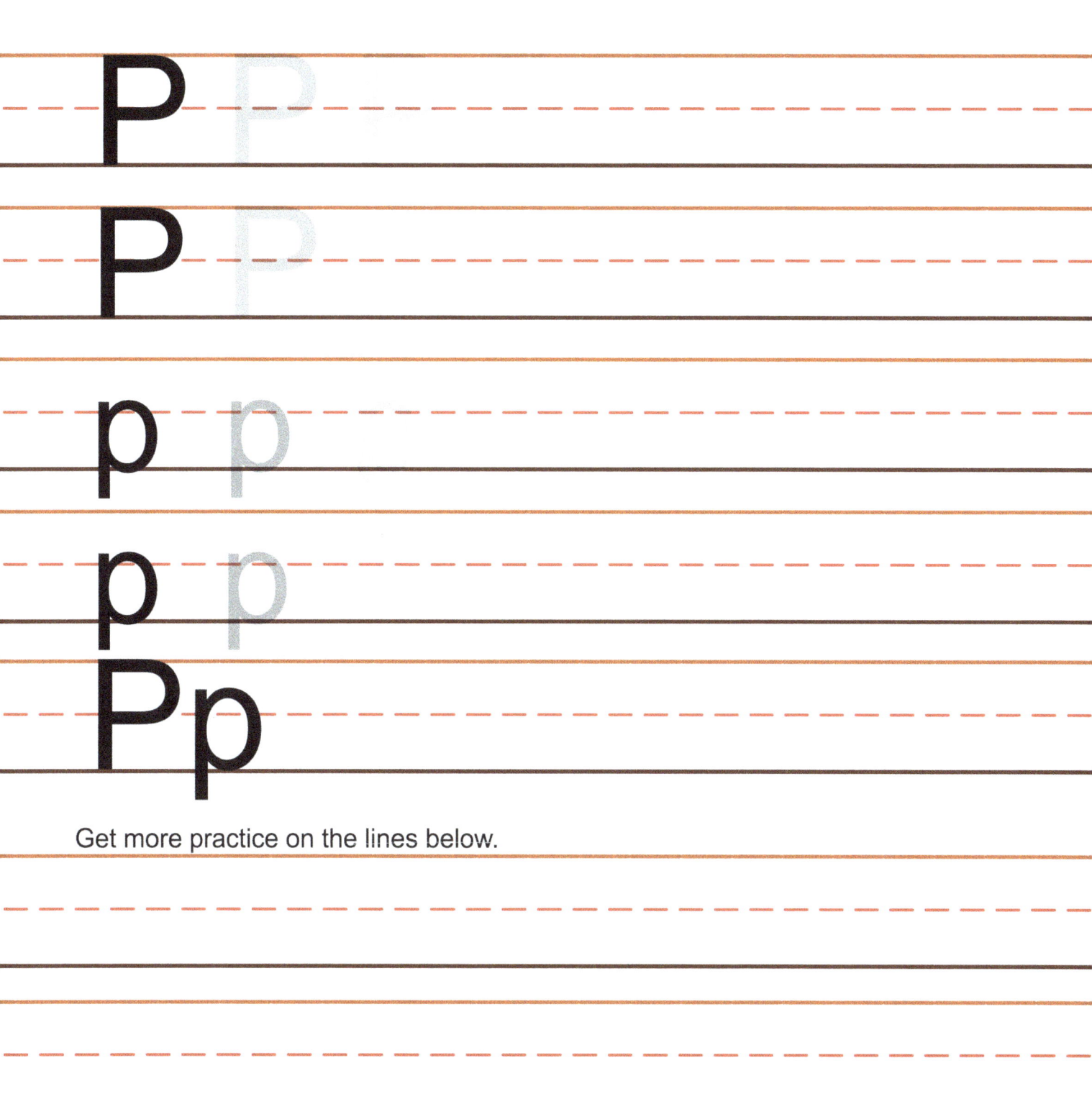

Color the letters.

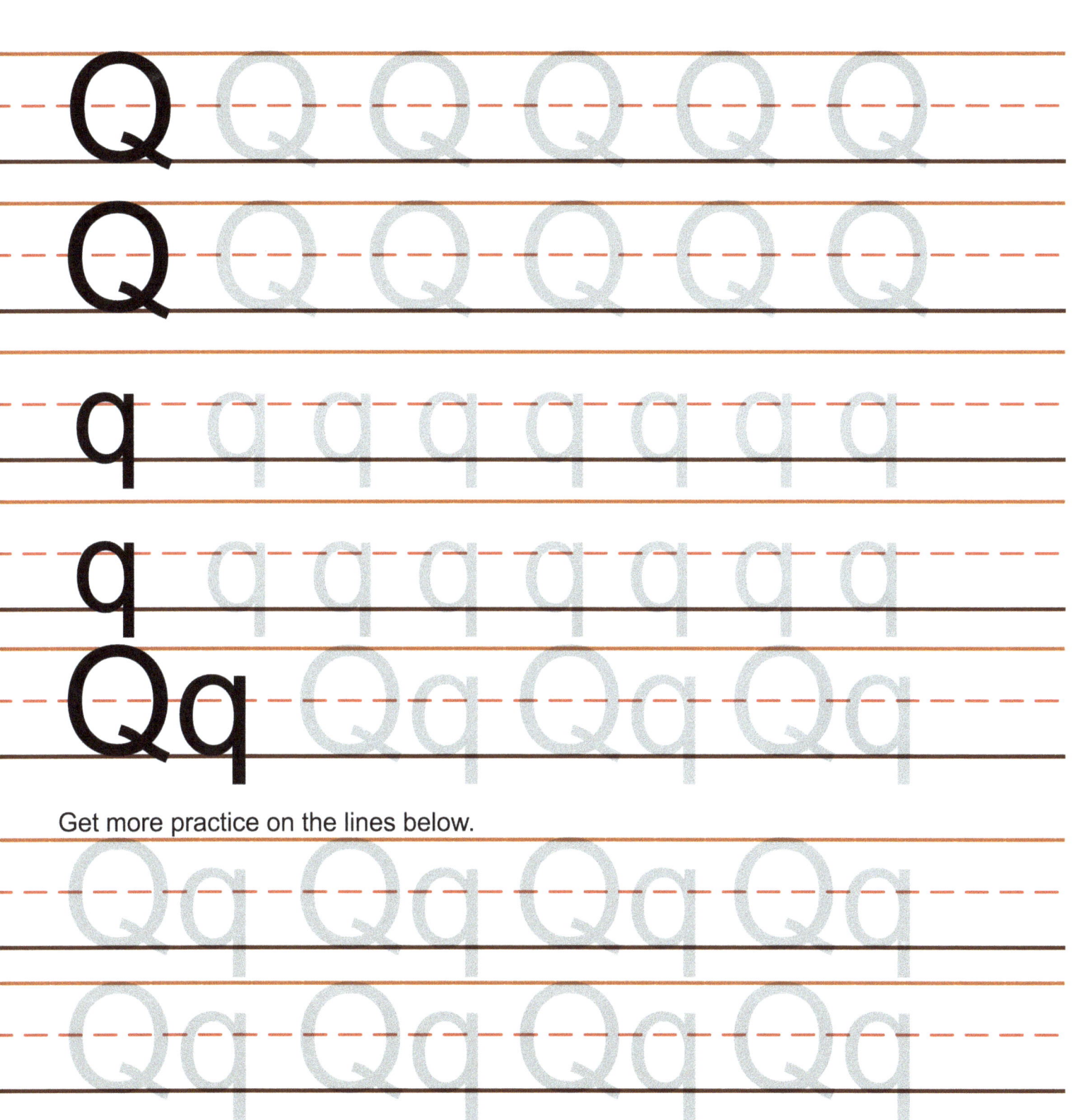

Get more practice on the lines below.

Get more practice on the lines below.

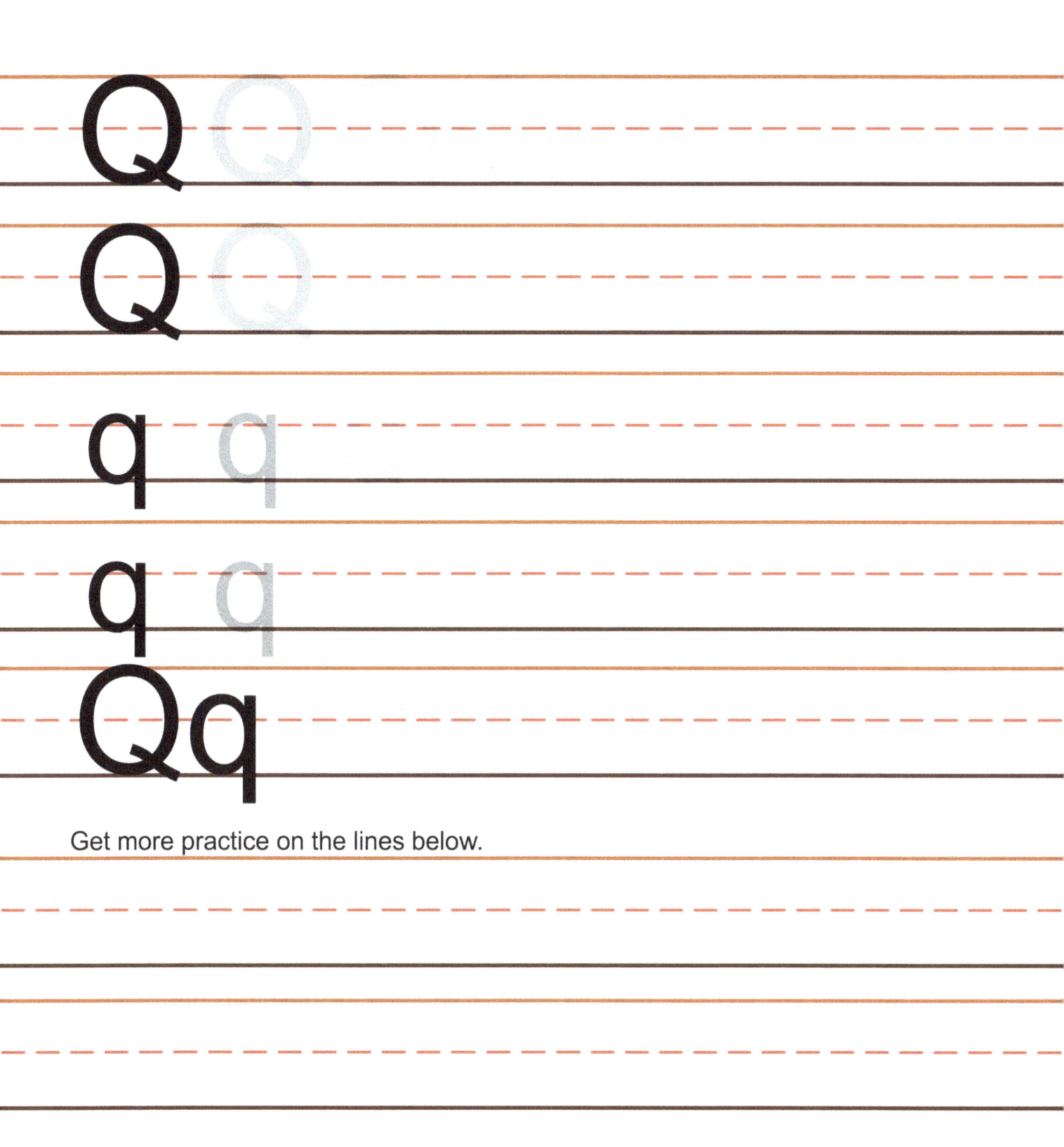

Get more practice on the lines below.

Color the letters.

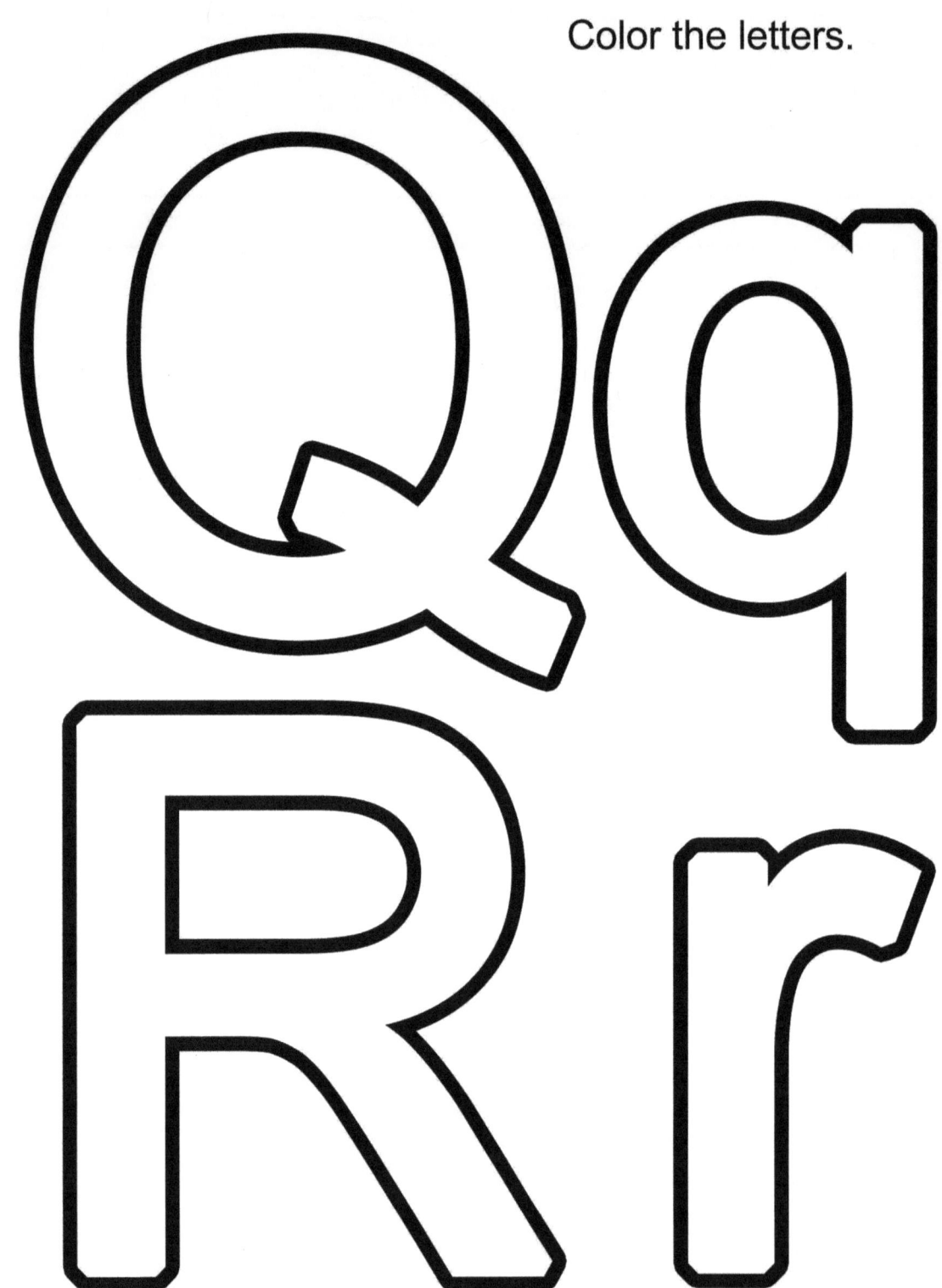

Get more practice on the lines below.

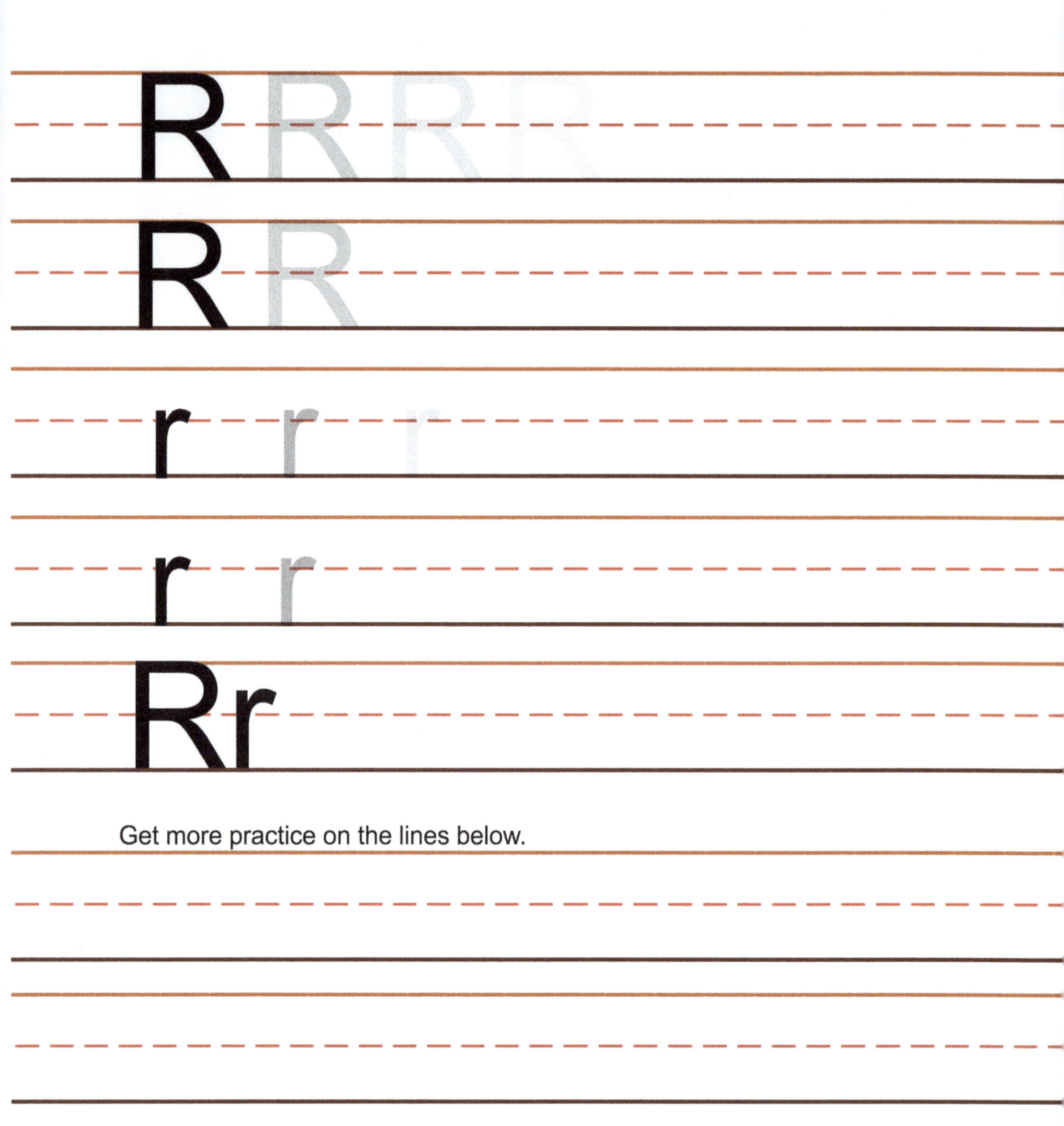

Get more practice on the lines below.

Get more practice on the lines below.

Color the letters.

Get more practice on the lines below.

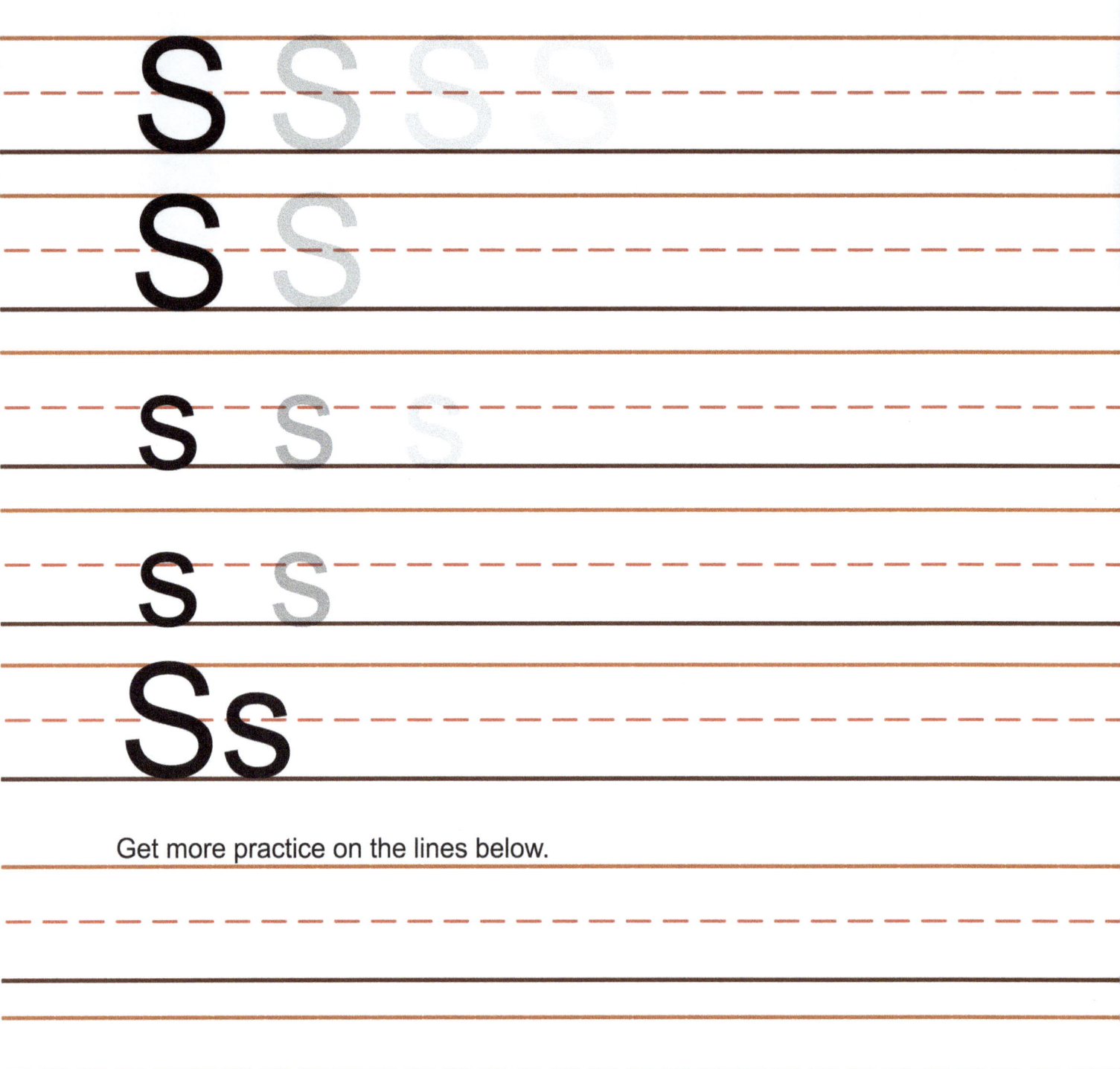

Get more practice on the lines below.

Get more practice on the lines below.

Color the letters.

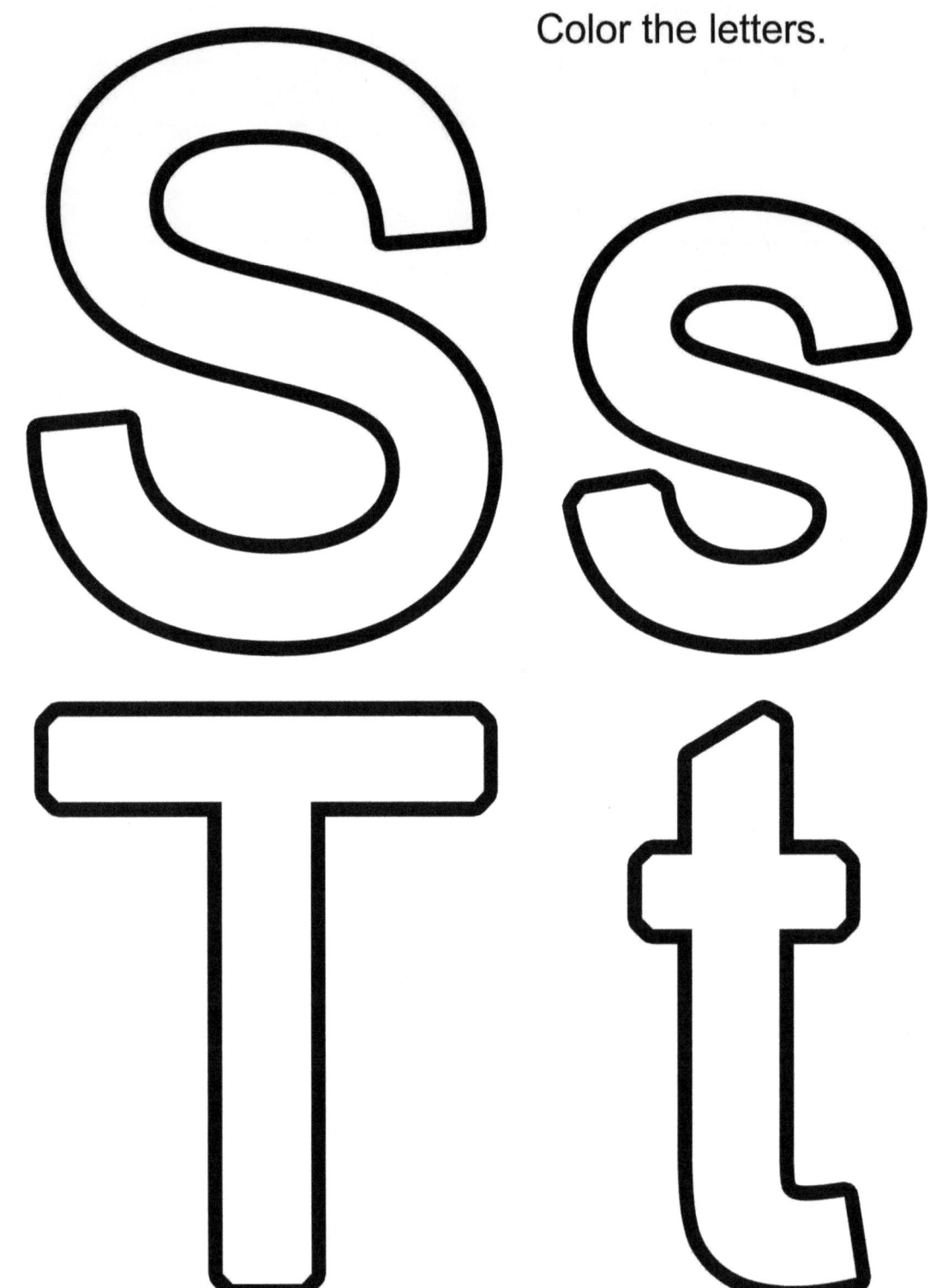

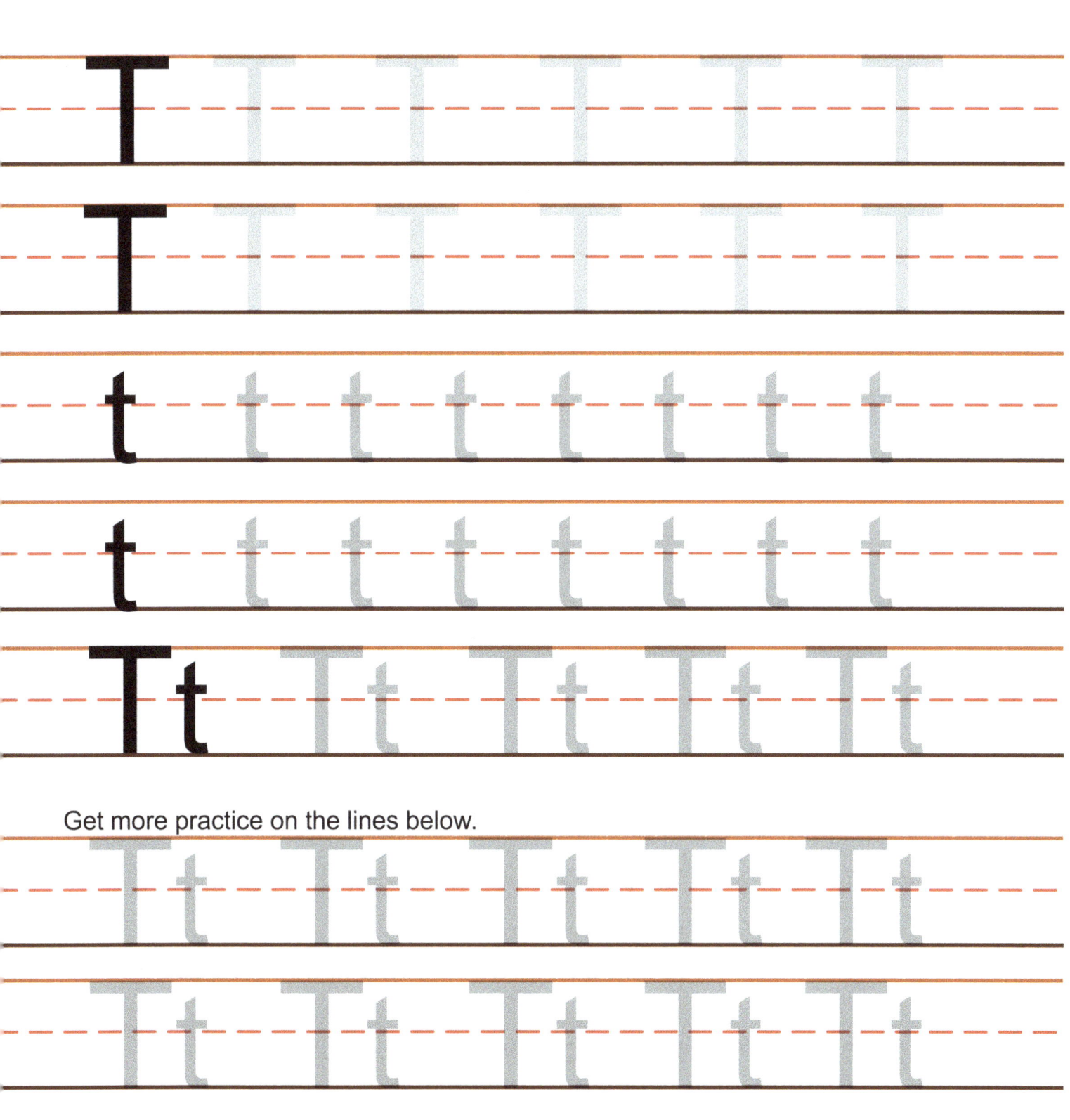

Get more practice on the lines below.

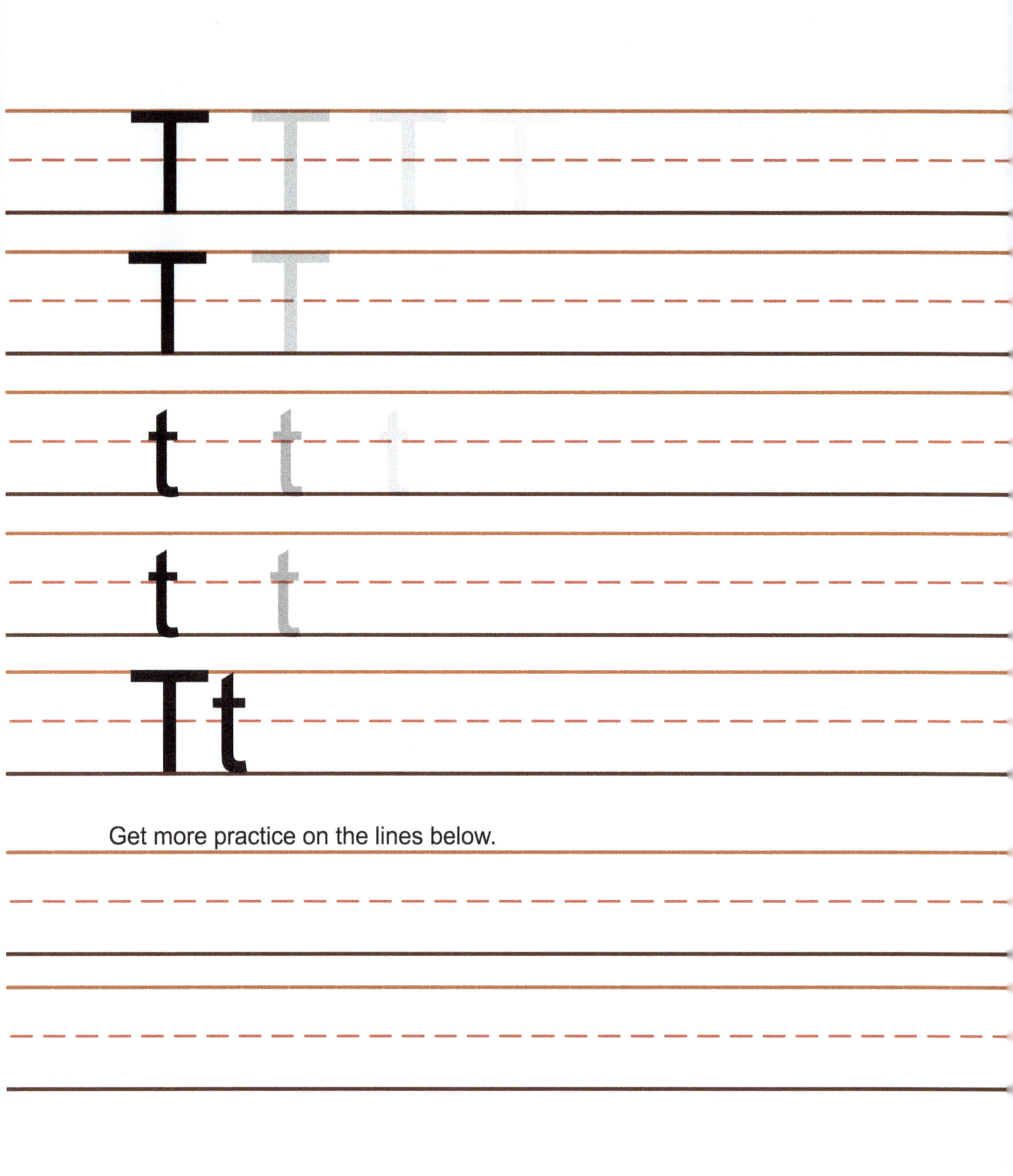

Get more practice on the lines below.

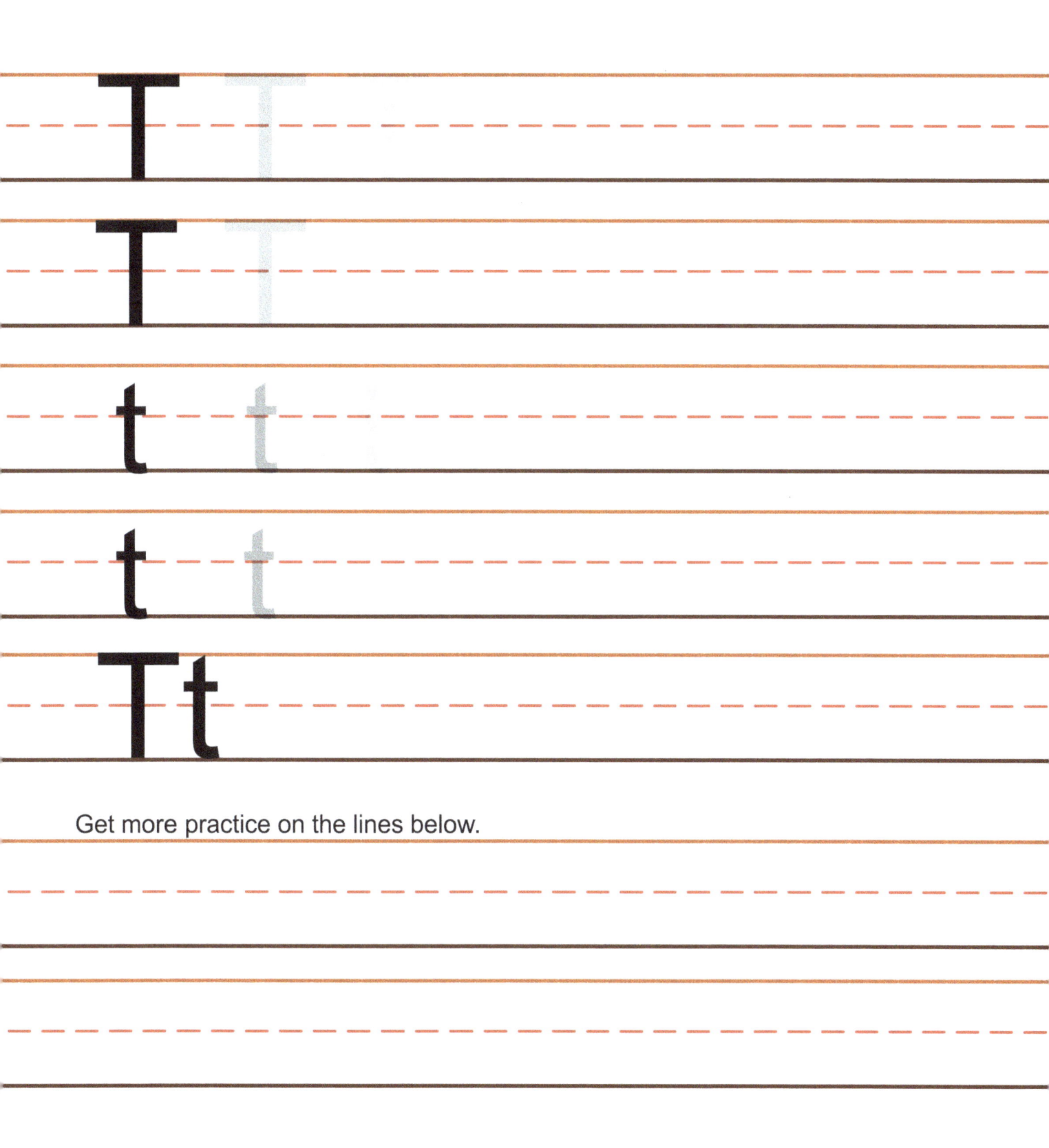

Get more practice on the lines below.

Color the letters.

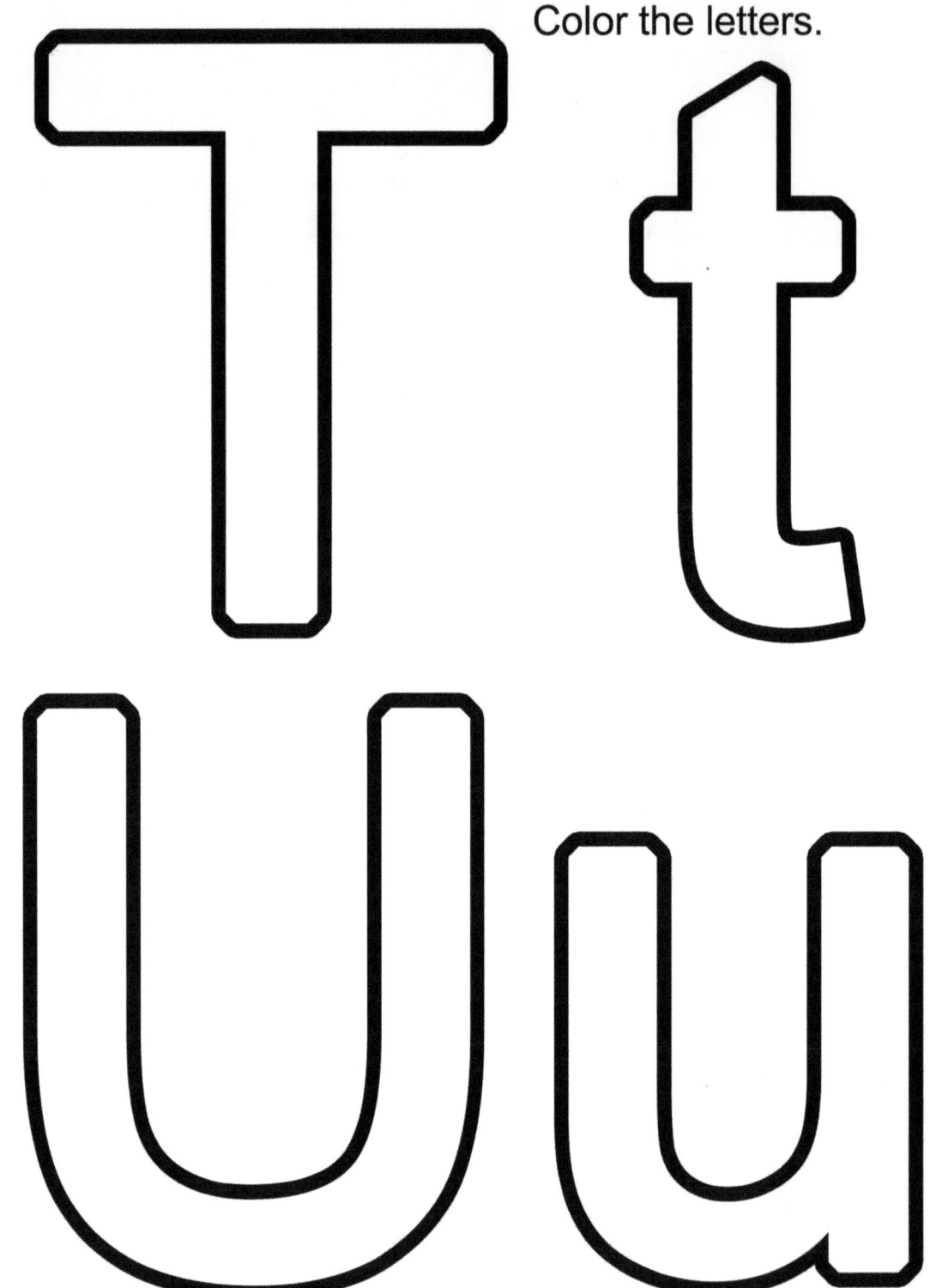

Get more practice on the lines below.

Get more practice on the lines below.

Get more practice on the lines below.

Color the letters.

Get more practice on the lines below.

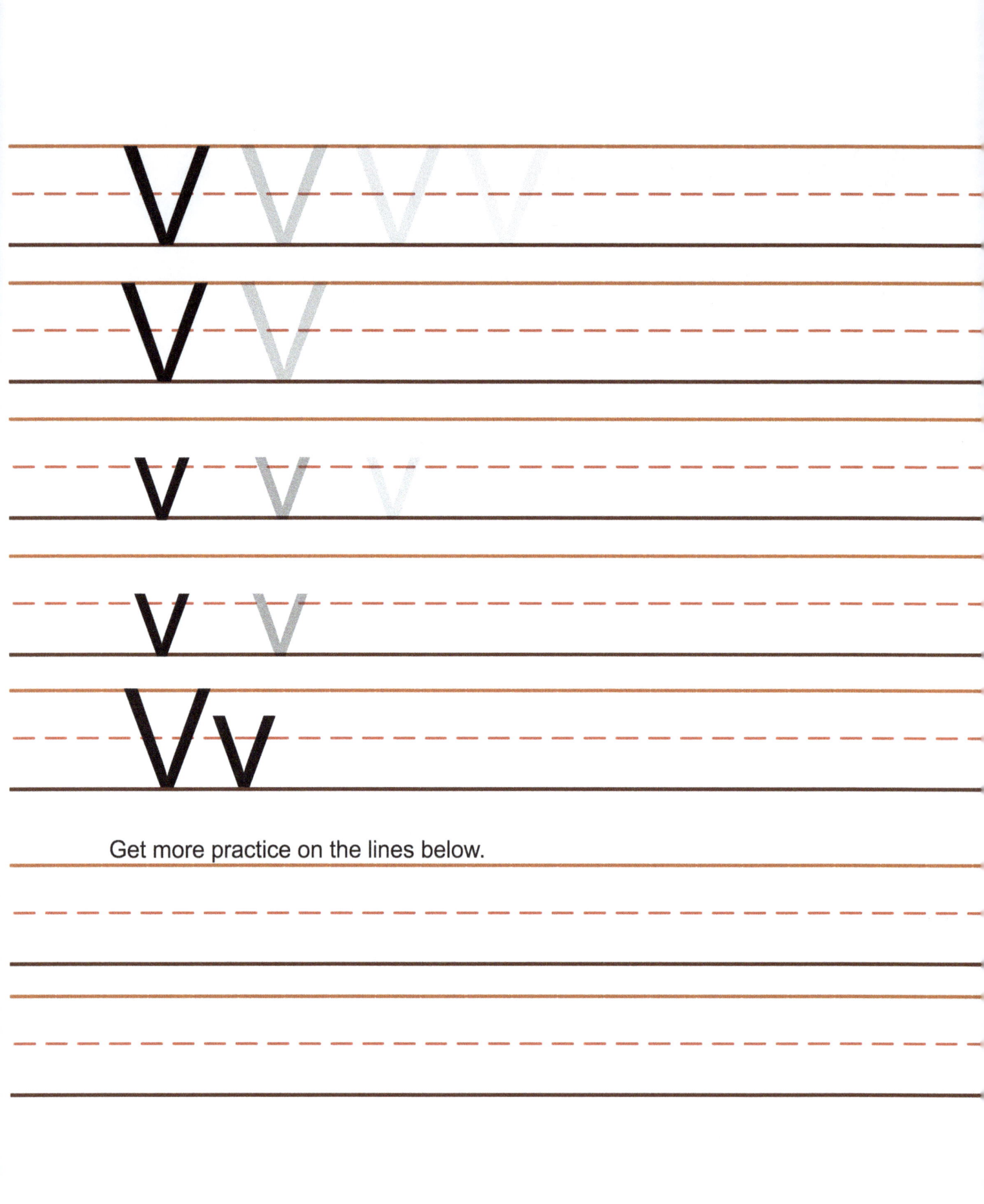

Get more practice on the lines below.

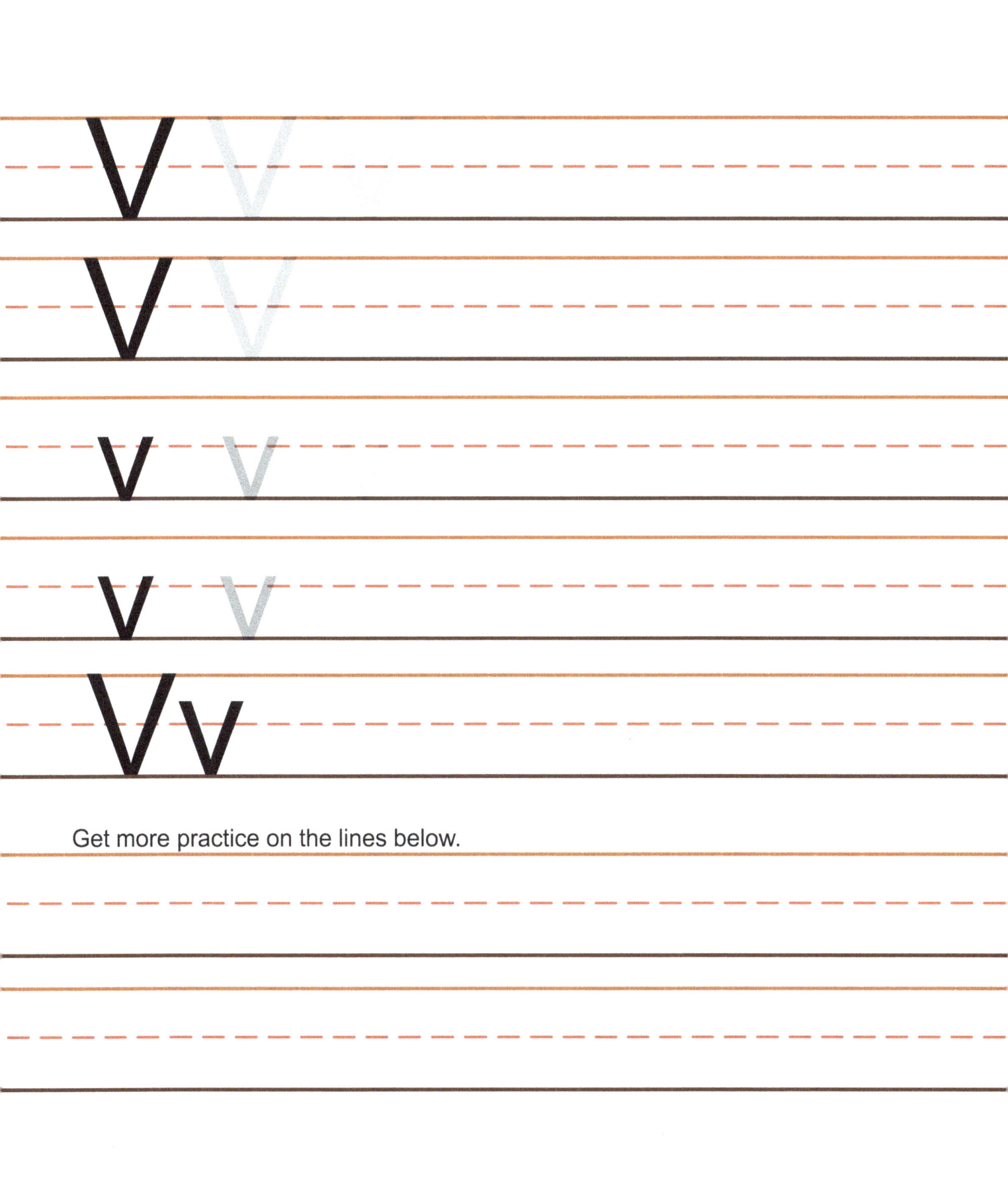

Get more practice on the lines below.

Color the letters.

Get more practice on the lines below.

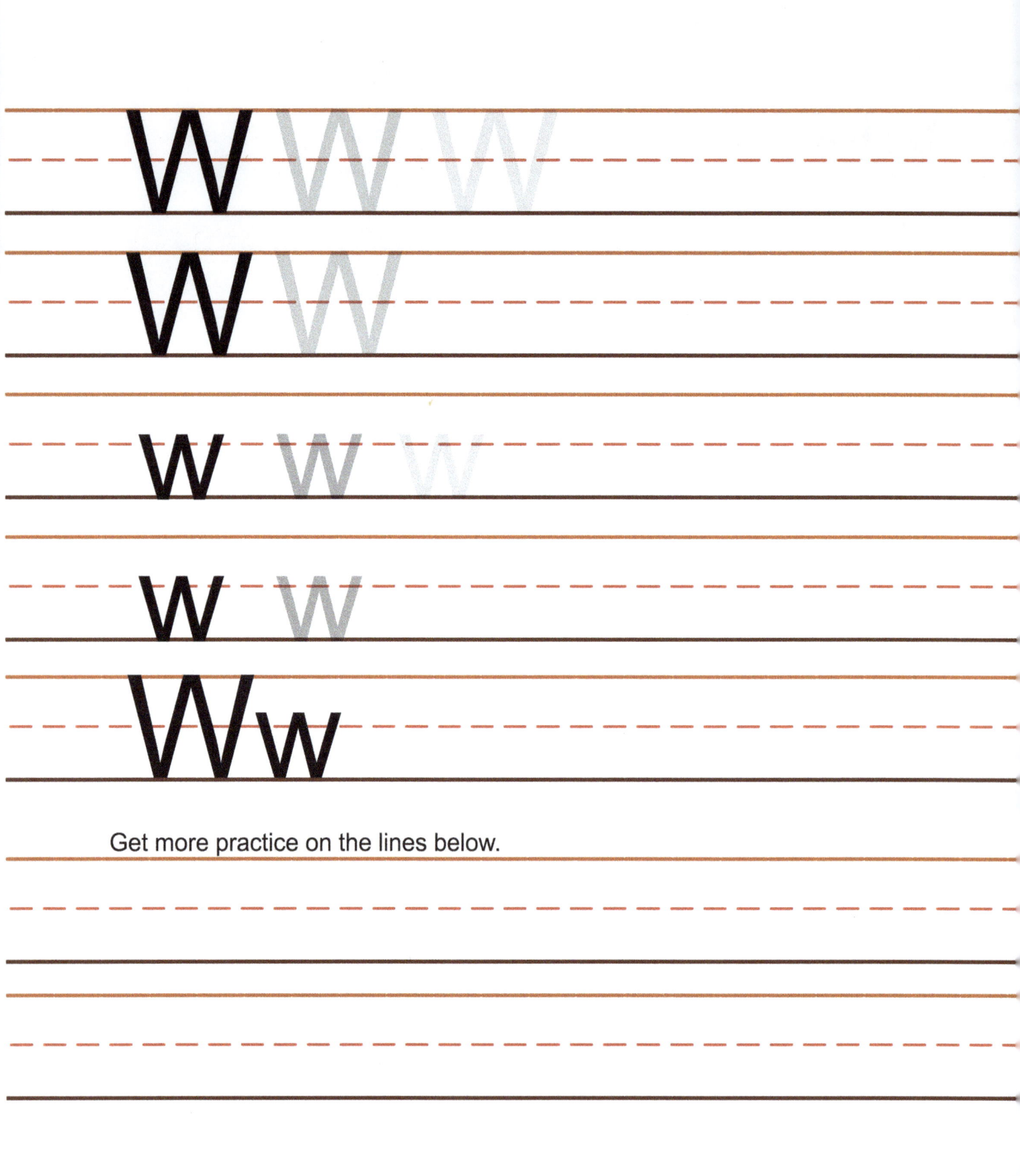

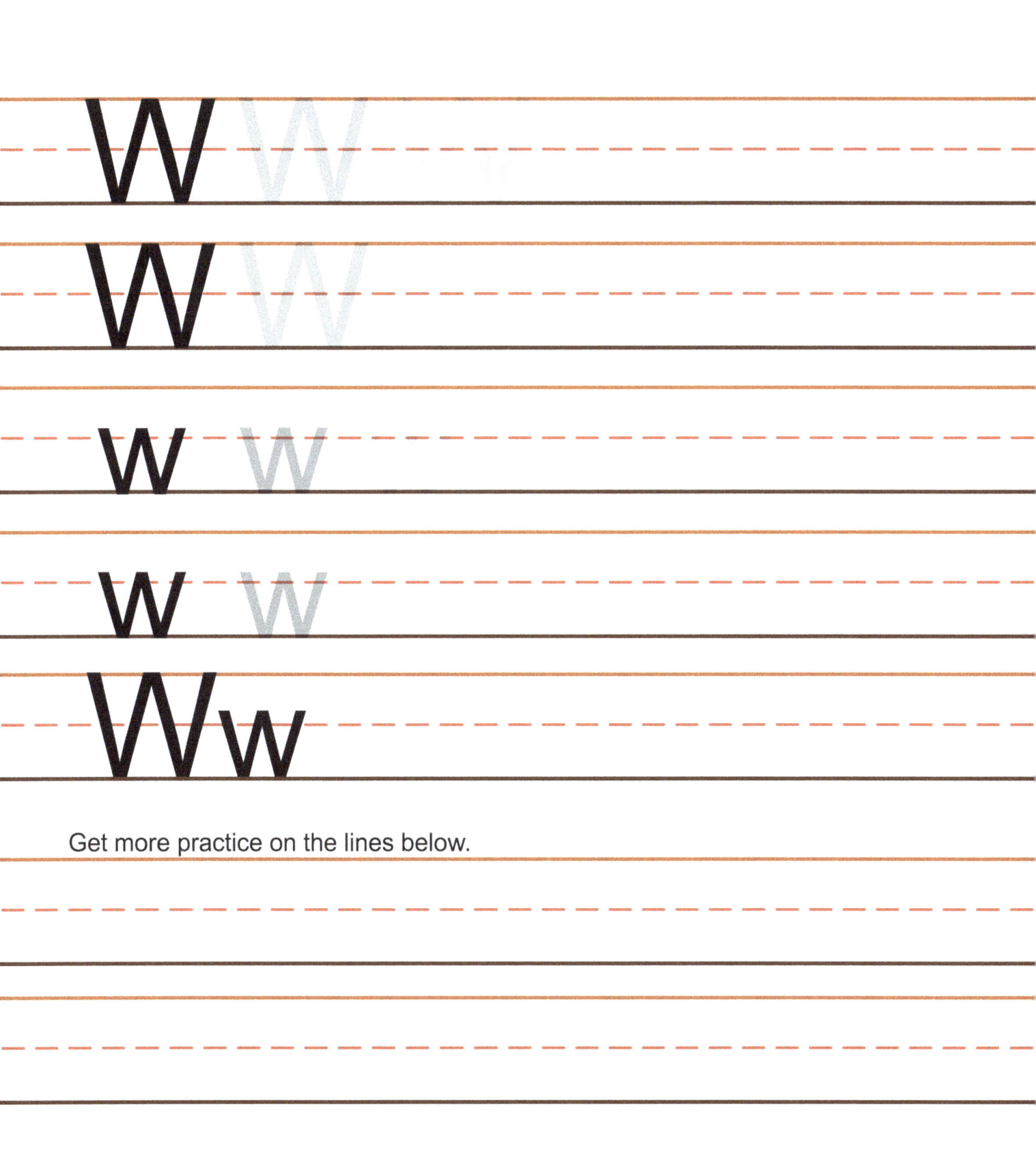

Get more practice on the lines below.

Color the letters.

Get more practice on the lines below.

Get more practice on the lines below.

Get more practice on the lines below.

Color the letters.

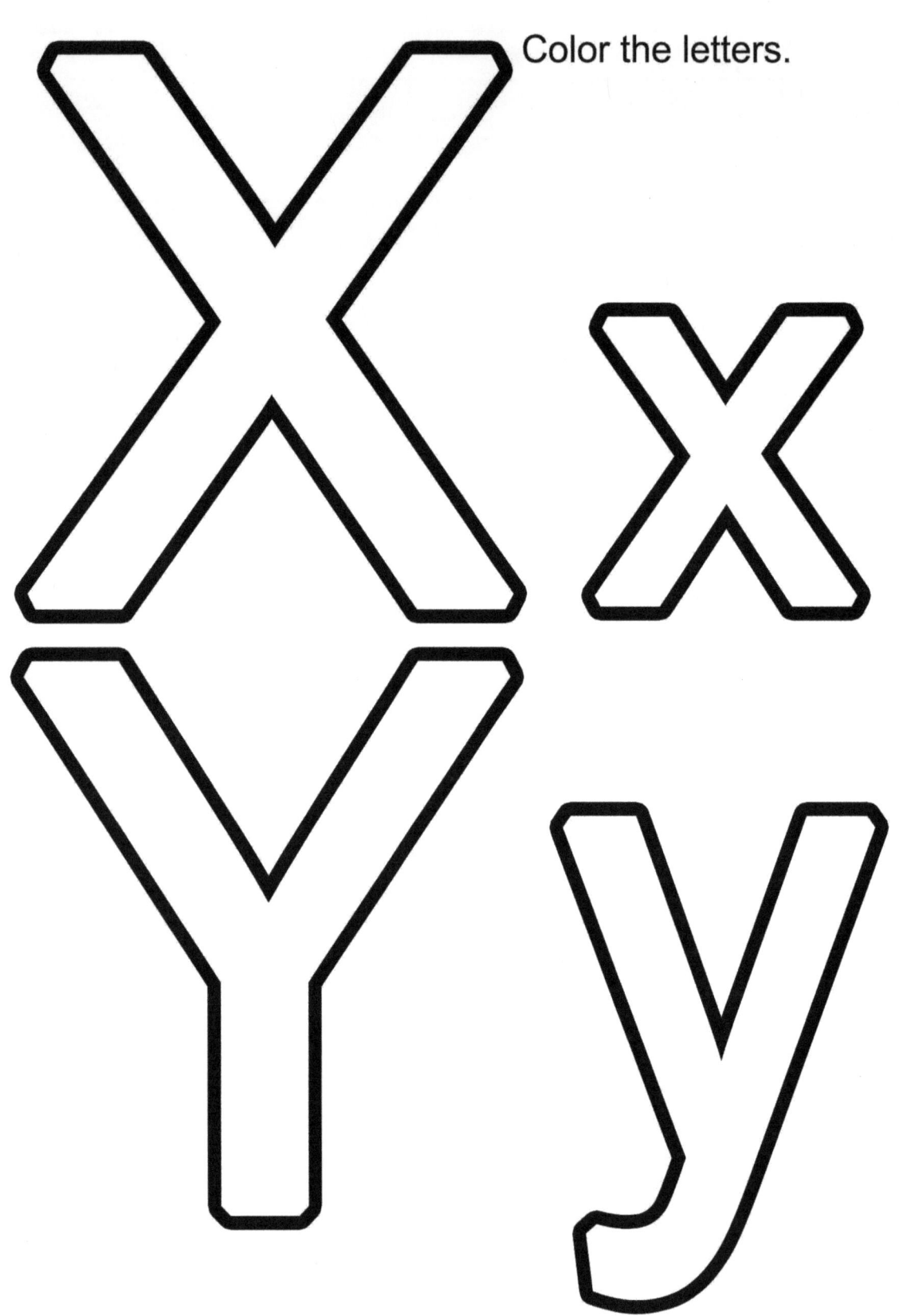

Get more practice on the lines below.

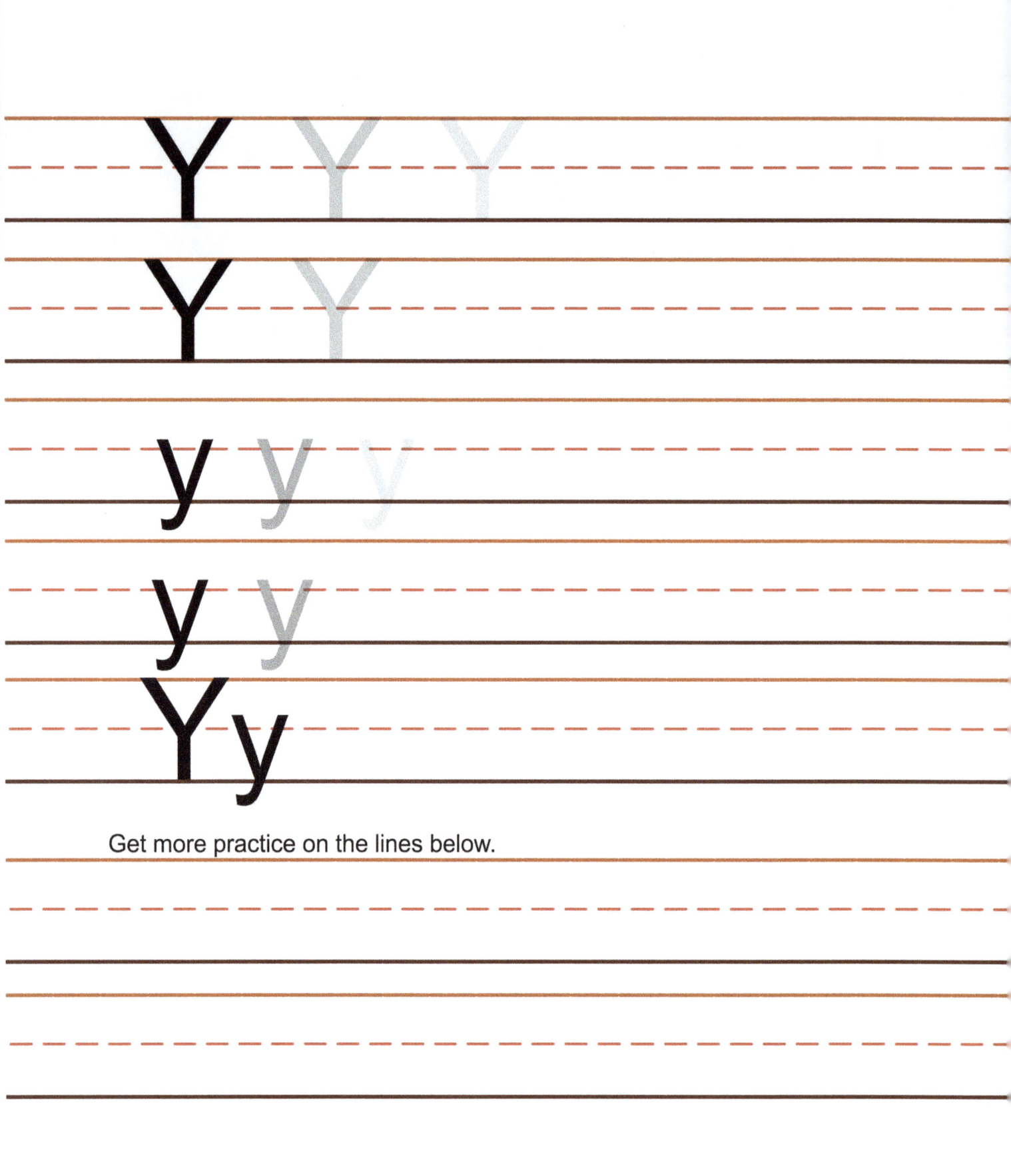

Get more practice on the lines below.

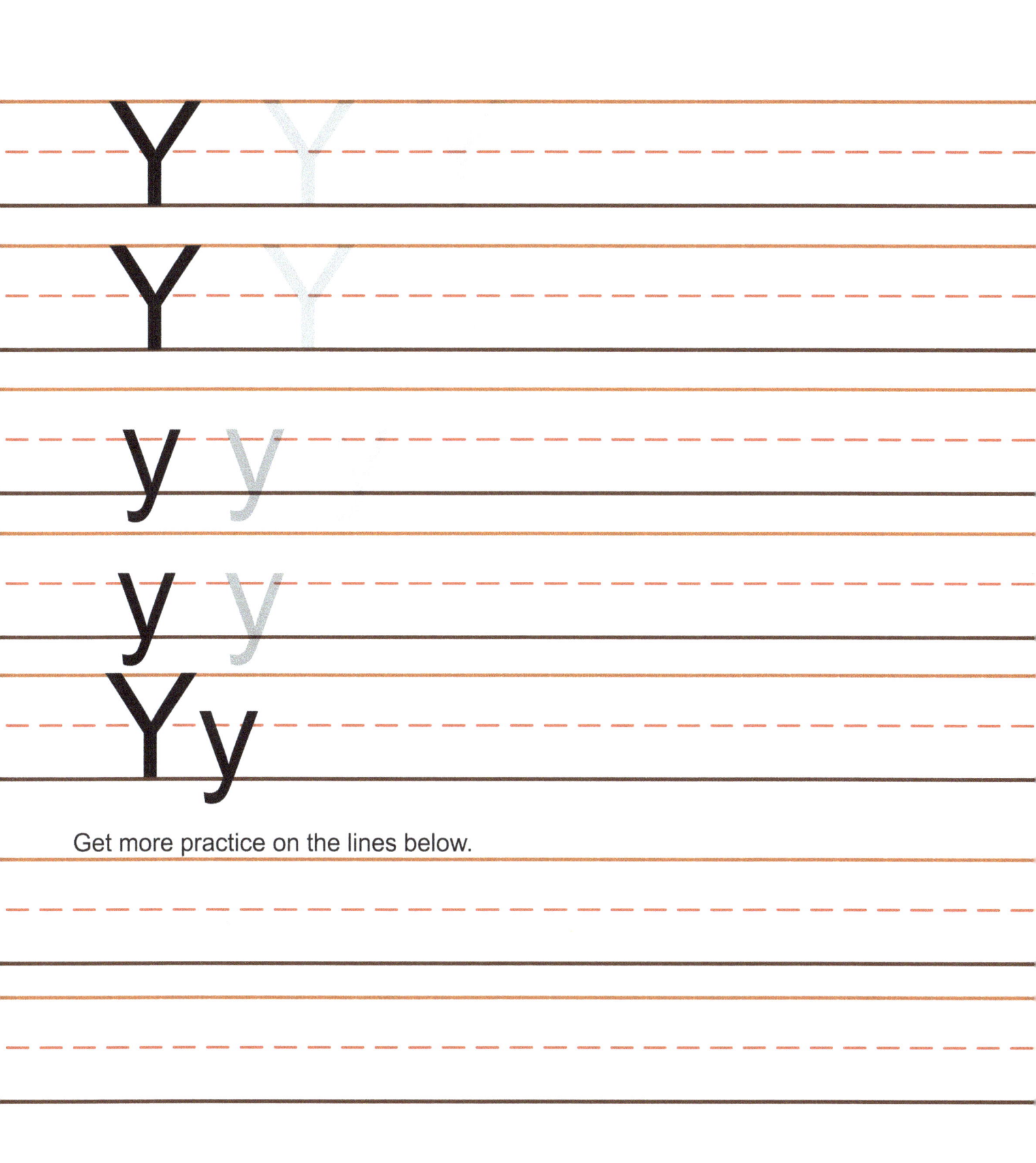

Get more practice on the lines below.

Color the letters.

Yy
Zz

Get more practice on the lines below.

Get more practice on the lines below.